William Ferguson Tamblyn

The establishment of Roman Power in Britain

William Ferguson Tamblyn

The establishment of Roman Power in Britain

ISBN/EAN: 9783744730181

Printed in Europe, USA, Canada, Australia, Japan

Cover: Foto ©ninafisch / pixelio.de

More available books at **www.hansebooks.com**

THE ESTABLISHMENT

OF

ROMAN POWER

IN BRITAIN.

BY

W. F. TAMBLYN, B.A.

Submitted in partial fulfilment of the requirements for the degree of Doctor of Philosophy, in the Faculty of Philosophy, Columbia University.

HAMILTON, ONT.:
PRINTED BY McPHERSON & DROPE.
1899

THE ESTABLISHMENT

OF

ROMAN POWER

IN BRITAIN.

BY

W. F. TAMBLYN, B.A.

Submitted in partial fulfilment of the requirements for the degree of Doctor of Philosophy, in the Faculty of Philosophy, Columbia University.

HAMILTON, ONT.:
PRINTED BY McPHERSON & DROPE.
1899

JULY. CALIFORNIA
LOS A. ELES LIBRARY

The Establishment of Roman Power in Britain.

CHAPTER I.

BRITAIN AND THE ROMAN WORLD.

When Julius Caesar entered upon the government of the province of Gaul, with the definite purpose of winning new conquests for the Roman People and military power and glory for himself, he identified personal interests with the needs of his country. On the one hand, conscious of his own greatness, he desired to do famous deeds, to be the first of Romans, and to link his name forever to those of Rome and Victory.[1] On the other hand, it was evident to Caesar that the security of Rome and her system was seriously threatened by the presence to the north and west of Italy of many large and vigorous independent tribes which had often beaten Roman armies, and had done much damage to Roman possessions and Roman interests in general.[2]

The Gauls in particular had been for centuries the terror of Italy.[3] Later the Germans, a still more dreadful apparition, had invaded Roman territory and were now threatening to spread over Gaul. At any moment Italy might again be assailed by Celtic or Teutonic barbarians. It was therefore necessary to extend the power of Rome over Gaul at least, to defend the Po at the Rhine, as one writer has expressed it,[4] in order that Italy might not fear the ravages of migrating barbarians. Convinced of this necessity, and of the power which would come to the

---

1. Sueton, Caesar 7. Cp. Dio XXXIX. 48.
2. Cp. J. R. Seeley, Essays on Roman Imperialism I. He points out the chief cause for the downfall of the Republic in the demand for military centralization against the barbarians.
3. Caes, B. G. I. 12; III. 20. Cic.,de Prov. Cons. 13 Sall. Jug. 114. Livy V, etc.
4. Jung, Roman. Landschaften, p. 191.

conqueror of the Republic's most redoubtable enemy, Caesar turned his face from the easy conquests of the east, which had attracted other Roman generals, and chose Gaul as the scene for his battles.

Other considerations must also have urged Caesar to this step. He must have felt instinctively that the empire of Rome, after its rapid extension in the East, needed balancing. If Rome was to remain the political centre of her empire, a counterpoise was required in the west to the dull weight of Asia.[1] Besides, the eastern provinces, with their Hellenic or Semitic traditions, offered no room for the free, unhindered development of a pure Roman civilization. Only in the west and north was Rome ever able to infuse her full spirit into the conquered nations, and become supreme by her intellectual and moral influence as well as by force of arms.[2] The extension of Roman civilization in the north-west was destined to prove the strongest bulwark of Italy against the outer barbarism. While the civilization of Rome endured and cemented fast the solid rampart of Gaul, Raetia, Noricum, and Pannonia, Italy needed no other walls to guard her culture against the assaults of German and Sarmatian hordes. Among the warlike but untutored Gauls, Caesar felt that an organic Romanism, a really sound, healthy expansion of Roman arts, trades, life and citizenship could be quickly realized by energetic and intelligent measures. Here, too, he could train an army which would not fail him in the future, while for the present the proximity of his province to the centre of the world enabled him to keep in touch with urban politics.

Accordingly, Caesar undertook a task which

---

1. Cp. Schiller, Geschichte der rom. Kaiserzeit I. §30.
2. That Caesar looked forward to Gauls becoming Roman citizens appears from his treatment of them (Dio XLIV. 42) and his numerous enfranchisements.

seemed enormous to his contemporaries.[1] His career in Gaul during the three years 58-56 B. C. was one of almost unbroken success. By the end of 56 the Roman power reached to the English Channel and the Atlantic Ocean. Caesar had an army of eight legions[2] in the finest condition, which not only overawed the Gauls, but had already taught the Germans respect for Rome. Leaving his army each winter quartered in the conquered territories, Caesar himself passed the winters when possible in Cisalpine Gaul, whence he could watch conveniently the course of events at Rome.[3] The gratitude of the Roman People for his successes[4] had already expressed itself in the form of a public thanksgiving of fifteen days (57 B. C.).[5] All eyes were turned in admiration upon the man who had crushed the inveterate enemies of the Republic and turned the tide of conquest northward.[6]

Now that the conquest of Gaul was practically finished, Caesar's further operations in the years 55-53 aimed chiefly at securing and consolidating what had been won.[7] After crossing the Rhine and demonstrating his strength to the Germans, Caesar turned his attention to the island of Britain.[8]

Up to the time of Caesar's invasion, Britain was almost wholly unknown to Romans.[9] The Gauls themselves, with the exception of a few traders, knew nothing of the island to the north of them.[10] Britain was

1. Catullus XI. 11. Cic. De Prov. Cons. 13. 14.
2. Caes. B. G. V. 8.
3. Caes. B. G. V. 1.
4. Cic. De Prov. 16.
5. Dio XXXIX. 5.
6. Cic. De Prov. Cons. 13. Dio XLIV. 42. Appian B. C. II. 73, 134.
7. Peter : Romische Geschichte p. 390.
8. Caes., B. G. IV. 20.
9. Diodorus Sic. III. 37. Plutarch, Caesar 23. Dio XXXIX. 50 ; LXII. 4.
10. Caes. IV. 20.

almost cut off from the rest of the world.[1] Some slight traffic however, especially in tin,[2] seems to have been carried on with the inhabitants of the south coast of England by venturesome traders even in quite early times. The Massiliot Pytheas probably visited Britain in the fourth century B. C.[3] From his Book of Travels the Pseudo-Aristotle perhaps derived his knowledge of the two British Isles, which he called Albion and Ierne.[4] Later on Polybius refers to the production of tin in the British Isles.[5] But the really historic discovery of Britain was made by Caesar.[6] Before him the Romans knew about as much of Britain as the people of Western Europe knew 900 years ago of Greenland.

Long before Caesar's appearance in Gaul various grand movements of peoples on the continent had forced divisions of the Celtic race to seek new homes beyond the Strait of Dover. Settling successively in Britain the several instalments of invaders pushed the previous populations westward and northward.[7] The last of these waves of invasion had flowed over the southeastern part of the island not very long before the time of Caesar.[8]

But there was no live intercourse between Britain and the continent.[9] Even the merchant traders whom

1. Vergil, Eccl. I. 67. Catull. XI. 12. Horace, Carm. I. 35, 29. Cic. N. D. II. 34, etc.
2. Diod. Sic., V. 38, says much tin was exported from Britain. But it was probably no large amount. Certainly the British tin mines were little worked during the Roman occupation. See Haverfield in Arch. Journ. XLIX. p. 178. Cp. Strabo (IV. 5, 2) who knows of no export of tin from Britain.
3. See Elton, Origins of English History, Ch. I.
4. Aristotle, De Mundo 3.
5. Polyb. III. 57. The Cassiterides of Hdt. (III. 115), Diod. Sic. (V. 38), Pliny, Strabo, Mela, &c., are of course no longer identified with Britain or the Scilly Islands. They lay off the coast of Spain.
6 Cp. Nouveau Dict. de Geographie Universelle s. v. Angleterre.
7. Cp. Rhys, Celtic Britain, Ch. 1.
8. Caes. B. G. II. 4. 7. Cp. V. 12.
9. Strabo II, 5, 8. Caesar (III. 8) says of the Veneti that they are far in advance of the other Gauls in navigation, and are wont to sail to Britain. That is, it was an unusual achievement to sail to Britain.

Caesar called to give him information, could tell him nothing as to the size of the island, the numbers and character of its inhabitants or the best harbors.[1] The Britons themselves seem to have been by no means a seafaring people. They simply received the foreign traders on their shores and took their copper, their manufactured wares, weapons, pottery and trinkets[2] in exchange for British tin or furs. The help therefore which Britons are said[3] to have given to the Veneti and other Gallic tribes in their struggles with Caesar must be regarded as quite mythical. The only way in which the insular Celts could show sympathy with their continental brethren was to receive hospitably a few refugees from Gaul, which passive assistance they seem to have actually rendered.[4] The Germans over the Rhine stood guilty before Caesar of the same misdemeanor, in a far higher degree.[5] The isolation of Britain appears from the statements of all the earliest writers about it. The Pseudo-Aristotle speaks of Britain as beyond the Celts. Strabo makes a sharp distinction between Keltike and Brettanike.[6] He also contrasts the Britons with the Keltoi more than once, though he has learnt from Caesar that they are much like the Keltoi.[7] No one knew in those days that the Britons were themselves Celts, speaking the language of the Celts. The utter ignorance of the Gauls about Britain and the English Channel is shown finally by the fact that Caesar found no pilots acquainted with the peculiar nature of the tides and the varying course of

---

1. B. G. IV. 20. The argument that the merchants refused to tell Caesar what they knew is as worthless as the assumptions made about the concealment of the Cornish tin trade from the Romans.
2. Caes. V. 12. Diodor. Sic. V. 21, 22.
3. Caes. IV. 20 ; III. 9.
4. Caes. II. 14.
5. Caes. IV. 16 ; V. 2.
6. Strabo, IV. 4 and 5.
7. Strabo IV. 5. 1-3.

the currents in the channel, who could have conducted his fleet with accuracy and expedition to the British shore. As it was, Caesar lost time and incurred great dangers in both expeditions owing to lack of information about these things.[1]

It has been assumed by many, *first*, that Caesar was deeply impressed, not only by a close intercourse and the racial ties between Britons and Gauls, but also by the common religious feeling of insular and continental Celts, connected with a Druidic system which had its headquarters in Britain; and, *secondly*, that the Gauls could not have been reconciled to Roman rule while their cousins and co-religionists in Britain remained free.[2] But it has just been shown that the Britons had scarcely any intercourse with the mainland. From this isolation alone it would seem almost certain that there was no community of religious feeling between them and the Gauls. Caesar was informed that the Druidic theology and ritual which he found in Gaul had originated in Britain. He says that young Gauls wishing to become fully equipped Druids went there to study at the headquarters or university of the order.[3] But it is impossible to believe that Caesar was not misinformed in this, as he was about certain features of the Hercynian Forest, and about the marriage customs among the Britons. Probably the Gallic Druids themselves were responsible for Caesar's error. Like many other philosophies, that of the Druids was given out by its professors to have come from beyond the seas, in order to surround it with greater sanctity.[4] The British Isles

---

[1]. Caes. IV. 23, 29; V. 8. Cp. Appian B. C. II. 150 on the isolation of Britain. See Freeman's Historical Essays, Fourth Series No. 9. "Alter Orbis."
[2]. Mommsen, Provinces of the Roman Empire, I. pp. 188-189. Merivale Vols. I and VI. Huebner, Römische Herrschaft in Westeuropa, p. 9.
[3]. B. G. VI. 13.
[4]. Cp. Ammianus XV. 9. 4, where part of the Gauls are said by the Druids to have come from "extimis insulis." Cp. also the "White Island" of the Brahmins.

which were almost fabulous before Caesar's time, and which seem to have been the Druidic Islands of the Blest,[1] were naturally seized upon as the sacred source of the science of the Druids. Or possibly the island to which would-be Druids went to study was somewhere close to the Gallic coast, like the one referred to by Strabo,[2] but confused by Caesar with Britain.[3] There is no ground whatever for supposing that either national or religious ties subsisted to unite the people of Britain and Gaul in resistance to the Romans. As for Caesar's own impressions, he evidently troubled himself little about any religious connection between Britons and Gauls, or he would have made more than the passing allusion to it which appears merely in the course of his short account of Druidism,[4] and quite apart from considerations of foreign policy. Surely he would have noticed this religious union in his description of the people, had it existed.[5]

The story of the young men traveling to Britain—or Anglesey, as some will have it—in pursuit of truth and knowledge, is a very pretty one, but it must be classed with other fairy tales which sprang up in antiquity about the unknown mysterious gem of the ocean at the world's western edge. Some believed that Britain was a land where the precious electrum could be obtained.[6] Stories were rife about treasures of gold and pearls unappreciated by British savages.[7] Caesar and others credited the Britons as well as other nations of the far north with a community of

---

1. Cp. Pelloutier, Histoire des Celtes II. 185-187.
2. Strabo IV. 4, 6.
3. The story quoted with approval by Strabo l. c. from Artemidorus of an island near Britain in which certain magic rites were celebrated may also be compared.
4. B. G. VI. 13.
5. For further discussion of "British Druidism" see Chapter III.
6. Pliny XXXVII. 11.
7. Dio XXXIX. 53.

wives little higher than bestial.[1] Strabo charges the Hibernians with cannibalism.[2]

These ancient fables about Britain yield only to the more elaborate inventions of modern times. Some have traced the philosophy of the Brahmins to the "White Island" of the west—Britain of course. Myfyr Morganwg says, "That the Druids of Britain were Brahmins is beyond the least shadow of a doubt."[3] The inspired vision of others sees the ten lost tribes of Israel wandering off to Britain, where at last forsooth they stay their steps perforce. Successors of the Hebrew Prophet allude slyly to Britain as the stone that fell from the mountain and filled the whole earth. While the vision of the ancients was somewhat restricted as to geographical sweep, they nevertheless succeeded in turning out romances as unworthy of belief as any of these modern hariolations.[4]

When, therefore, Caesar determined late in the summer of 55 B. C. to make a descent upon Britain, it was not because any close connection between Britons and Gauls led him to believe that for the complete pacification of Gaul the conquest of Britain was necessary.[5] Nor is there reason to suppose that he was following out any definite plan for the subjugation and annexation to Rome of the Celtic race as a whole. Only a modern philologist or ethnologist could entertain such a fancy. Certainly the aid which Caesar alleges to have come to the Gauls from Britain is not worth considering. It is put forward only as a pretext, and may be a part of Caesar's supposed self-justification.

1. Caes. V. 14.
1. Strabo IV. 5, 4.
3. Quoted by Bonwick, Irish Druids, p. 8.
4. For still more childish inventions see Gutschmid, Kleine Schriften Vol. II, p. 606, and Vine, Caesar in Kent, ch. I. and II.
5. Cp. Froude, Caesar pp. 296-298.

The first real motive of Caesar's sudden determination to invade Britain was the same as that which led him to cross the Rhine. He intended to show the hapless barbarians that neither the swift, wide river, nor the ocean itself could stop the ponderous, certain progress of the Roman legion.[1]

As Rome had crossed the Mediterranean Sea, so she could as easily draw Germany and Britain within the sphere of her dominion. Like other Romans of his day, Caesar had no clear idea of an ultimate hard and fast limit to the advance of the legions and the fasces of the magistrate.[2] Not only did the safety of Italy and the civilized world demand at least a universal recognition of the hegemony of Rome, but commercial interests made the middle class of Roman citizens eager for the opening up of new regions for their enterprise. While the conservative senatorial party was for many reasons inclined to go easy in the matter of foreign conquest,[3] the lower classes were all for a forward policy. Caesar and his successors, Augustus and Tiberius Caesar, reversed the old senatorial system which surrounded the limited sphere of actual Roman administration by clusters of more or less dependent states. They developed more rapidly the Roman and Liberal idea that distinctions of patricians and plebeians, Roman and Latin rights, Italy, the provinces, free and federated states should be gradually levelled, and Rome herself should grow out until conterminous with the limits of her influence.[4] Gaul was to be an organized Roman province, governed by Roman magistrates, and not a collection of more or less free states recognizing Rome's supremacy. But for the consolidation of

1. Cp. Josephus B. J. VI. 6.
2. Vergil VI. 794, 851-853. Dio Cassius XLIV. 43.
3. Cp. Jung, Rom. Landsch. p. 198.
4. Schiller I § 34, etc. Mommsen, Hist. IV. 650 ff. See Sueton. Caesar 28, cited by Arnold, Later Roman Commonwealth, p. 225.

Roman authority in Gaul, it was first of all necessary for Caesar to cut off from its peoples all hope of succor from outside.[1] The natural limits of the new province were clearly the Pyrenees, the Mediterranean Sea, the Alps, the Rhine, the English Channel and the Ocean.[2] Spain was already under Roman government. The Gauls could look for no help in that quarter. Only on the north and east could the spectacle of tribes still untamed to the Roman yoke meet their eyes.[3] And more than that, the German tribes across the Rhine were traditionally accustomed, when pressed for room, to look to the fertile plains of Gaul as their natural prey.[4] To prevent, therefore, German sympathy and aid from stiffening the resistance of Gaul, to put a stop to the German tendency to cross the Rhine into Roman territory,[5] and probably also, in accordance with the new principle of gradually extending Rome's administration over the whole domain of her suzerainty and for military ends as well,[6] to prepare the way for a Roman province in Germany with the territory of the Ubii as its nucleus, Caesar crossed the Rhine twice (55 and 53 B. C.) in force, frightened the Suevi into their forest fastnesses, and took hostages from the Ubii. Similarly, to cut off any forlorn hope that his enemies might entertain of a refuge in Britain, Caesar crossed the straits twice, took hostages and tribute from the Britons, and enrolled many of their tribes, like the Ubii, under the suzerainty of Rome.

The mingling of commercial considerations with the more strictly political objects is clear from the large

---

1. Cp. Ranke, Weltgesch. II. 251
2. B. G. I. 1.
3. Cp. Tac. Agric. 24 end, of the Britons.
4. Caes. I. 31 *ff.* ; IV. I.
5. Caes. IV. 16.—Caesar evidently recognizes the Rhine as the boundary of Gaul, but not of the Empire, potentially.
6. See above p. 1 and also ch. IV.

number of private vessels that accompanied Caesar's armada in 54 B.C.[1] Great things were expected of the British Eldorado. Wild rumors of its wealth, its pearls,[2] and gold and silver, lead and tin, stirred the minds of all classes.[3] Thousands of Roman speculators and promoters were ready to spring upon these mineral treasures as soon as the legions should open up the country.[4] The size of Britain had been greatly exagerated from the days of Pytheas of Massilia. One writer even declared, " The world of the Britons is as large as our own."[5] Roman citizens awaited the result of Caesar's venture with excitement.[6] The irresistible enchantment of the unknown drew Caesar on to dispel the mists that hid the cliffs of the expected new world from the eye of civilization. If anticipations had been realized, Caesar would probably not have let Britain go. It would have been quickly converted into a Roman province and developed in the interests of Roman capital and trade.[7]

Many other motives combined to recommend the British expedition to Caesar. His political position was just at this time extremely precarious.[8] A successful descent upon the unknown distant island, victories wrapt in a halo of mystery were sure to strengthen his popularity with the masses at Rome. It has been said that in this attempt to rival Alexander the Great's invasion of India, Caesar ran a tremendous risk of losing his hold on the new conquests which he left behind him. But this is hardly true. The recent

1. Caes. V. 8. Though the well-informed were becoming aware of Britain's poverty in precious metals (See Cic. ad Att. IV. 16).
2. Plin. H. N. IX. 57. Sueton. Caes. 47.
3. Dio XXXIX. 53. Cic. ad Fam. VII. 7. etc.
4. Cp. Diodor. Sic. V. 36 on the Spanish mines.
5. Josephus B. J. II. 16. Cp. Velleius II. 46 " alterum paene orbem."
6. Cic. ad Fam. VII. 6 ; ad Q. F. II. 16.
7. Not at all as being a Celtic people.
8. Appian De R. G. 18.

cumulative disasters that had befallen the Gauls, and the awful destruction of the Usipetes and Tencteri, had for the time paralyzed even the courageous spirit of the Gauls.[1] This is shown by the sudden breakdown of the Morini, who humbly submitted to their conqueror in the summer of 55.[2] Caesar left plenty of force under his able lieutenant, Labienus, to prevent disturbances on the continent.

But more than even the statesman and politician is shown in Caesar's expedition to Britain. His own account of his experiences in the island, of its geography, inhabitants, climate and productions, reveals the same adventurous spirit and cultured desire of knowledge for its own sake that in our time led Baker to the sources of the Nile. The contemporaries of Columbus scarcely outdid the ecstasies of Cicero over the discovery of Britain.[3]

By appearing among the Britons, Caesar was not only securing his conquests in Gaul, and satisfying a natural curiosity about an unknown land from which huge spoils were expected, but he pointed out[4] and smoothed the way for the subsequent conversion of Britain into a Roman province. Whether Caesar himself, after his final return from Britain intended this result is very doubtful. To judge from the policy of Augustus, it would seem that the political aim which Caesar bequeathed to his heir was rather the consolidation of Roman administration tending towards uniformity throughout the empire, the only actual extension projected being in the direction of the River Elbe. After his two campaigns in Britain, Caesar was apparently convinced that this island would be a useless and

---

1. Cp. Froude, Caesar p. 290.
2. Caes. IV. 22.
3. Cic. ad Q. F. II. 16. Cp. Caesar himself quoted by Eumenius, Paneg. Constant. Caes. II.
4. Tac. Agric. 13.

costly acquisition for Rome in any event, and certainly not to be thought of for the present. It is true that here, as in Gaul, a fresh, unworked field invited Roman energy, capital and institutions. The British promised splendid material for the standing army of the empire. But Germany, with equal qualifications, lay nearer at hand, and besides fitted better into the empire as a whole,[1] which required an advance of its outposts to the Elbe, in order to shield Italy on the north from possible invasion and to shorten and simplify the long line of defences against barbarism. The British expeditions of Caesar therefore, undertaken partly in order to secure the Roman authority in Gaul and to strengthen Caesar's power and popularity, partly as a voyage of discovery and reconnoitre with a view to conquest if profitable, certainly not from a conviction of the necessity of adding Britain to the empire in any event, in view of racial and religious considerations,[2] resulted in a degree of disappointment, and for nearly a hundred years afterwards no serious thought occurred to any Roman emperor of subduing Britain to his sway.

1. Cp. Strabo II. 5. 8. He says Britain would be no *strategic* gain to the empire.
2. Cp. Peter, p. 390; Florus Epit. 45. Dio XLI. 32 and XLIV. 43 are no proof that Caesar intended to complete the conquest of Britain. These are only speeches. Cp. Dio XL. 4.

CHAPTER II.

CAESAR'S BRITISH EXPEDITIONS.

After his flying trip into Germany in the summer of 55 B. C., Caesar turned northward, and nothing loth to find fresh employment for his troops,[1] entered the territory of the Morini, who inhabited that part of the coast opposite Dover, with the intention of extending Roman influence to the large island across the channel.[2] As the season was far spent, he proposed simply to go there with a moderate force and take note of the inhabitants and geography of the country, and whether it would be worth subjugating. He could find out nothing from traders.[3]

While he made his preparations for the expedition, Caesar sent off C. Volusenus with a battleship to reconnoitre the British coast, pick out a suitable landing-place and learn everything he could. But several British tribes warned of Caesar's designs, partly by the approach of Volusenus, partly by traders and Gallic refugees, and advised of the irresistible might of Roman arms,[4] sent ambassadors to Caesar, promising hostages and submission to Roman authority. Caesar received them graciously, and sent back with them one Commius, a Gaul of prominence whom he had made king of the Atrebates.[5] Commius' orders were to visit the tribes, proselytize for Rome and proclaim Caesar's speedy

---

1. Cp. Merivale i. 481.
2. B. G. IV. 21.
3. B. G. IV. 20.
4. Dio XXXIX. 51.
5. B. G. IV. 21—"cuius auctoritas in his regionibus magni habebatur." Certainly "his regionibus" refers to northern Gaul, not to Britain. Or else Commius could have given Caesar information about Britain.

coming. Volusenus, without daring to land in Britain, soon returned, and reported what little he had seen of the coast.[1]

Shortly before he sailed Caesar received a sure proof of how his startling victories over the Germans had cowed the Gallic mind. The submission of the yet unconquered Morini greatly assisted the Roman general's arrangements. Finally, when all was ready, Caesar left the bulk of his army under his legates, Sabinus and Cotta, to attend to the refractory Menapii as well as those cantons of the Morini which had not yet submitted, and under Sulpicius Rufus a guard for Portus Itius from which he sailed.[2] Taking with him two legions, the seventh and tenth, without impedimenta,[3] Caesar embarked about the end of August[4] upon something more than eighty vessels. The cavalry he ordered to proceed to another port eight miles north of Portus Itius, where were seventeen vessels which had been unable to join the main fleet, and follow him without delay.[5]

Though the identification of Caesar's Portus Itius with Gesoriacum or Boulogne has been much disputed, it seems nevertheless to be fairly certain.[6] The argument of Von Goeler against Boulogne, that the passage thence was not the shortest to Britain, amounts to nothing. Caesar does not say that he went by the shortest route. While he states that from the territories of the Morini " erat brevissimus in Britanniam traiectus," he claims for the passage from Portus Itius only that it

[1] B. G. IV. 21.
[2] IV. 22. cp. V. 2 and Strabo IV. 5. 1 ; see Ridgeway in Journ. of Phil. XIX. p. 140, and Mommsen Hist. IV. 312 Note.
[3] IV. 30.
[4] See Goeler, Caesars Gallischer Krieg p. 165.
[5] IV. 23.
[6] Desjardins: Geographie de la Gaule romaine, vol. I. pp. 348 *f.* 371 *f.* Peskett: Journ. of Phil. XX. 191 *ff.* Bursian: Jahresbericht LXIV. (1890), p. 137. Napoleon III. Histoire de Jules Cesar, II. pp. 163-169.

was "commodissimus."[1] But it was Gesoriacum which proved a hundred years later "commodissimum" for the embarcation of Plautius' armament.[2] It always remained the best starting-point for an invasion of England from the continent. Napoleon assembled his flotilla at Boulogne in 1804. From Gesoriacum, Pliny measured the distance between Britain and Gaul.[3] Moreover, Boulogne is the only harbor in the ancient territory of the Morini, eight miles north of which is another harbor from which Caesar's cavalry could have sailed. Ambleteuse suits exactly.[4] The identification by Guest and Ridgeway of Wissant as the Portus Itius is supported by no convincing argument. Their interpretation of Kai in Strabo IV. 5. 1 (Kai to Ition) as implying "as well as the well known Gesoriacum," is not at all plausible. Kai merely adds one more starting-point to the four already mentioned by Strabo. Von Goeler's adoption of Calais[5] can not meet with favor, when it is remembered that Caesar sailed from Portus Itius in 55 B. C. as well as in the second expedition of the following year.

No doubt Volusenus was with Caesar, directing the course of the fleet. When on arriving below the cliffs of Britain the Romans descried the natives above, armed and making demonstrations which did not argue for the success of Commius' mission, Caesar laid before a council of war the information which Volusenus had been able to furnish and his own plan, which was to sail along to a flat, open beach where a landing would be less exposed to the missiles of the enemy.[6] Such a

[1]. B. G. IV. 21 ; V. 2.
[2]. Sueton. Claudius 17. Huebner R. H. W. p. 17.
[3]. H. N. IV. 30, cp. Mela III. 2.
[4]. Napoleon, Cesar II. 166.
[5]. Page 128.
[6]. B. G. IV. 23.

place was soon found, near Romney, west of Hythe.[1] Here, in spite of great difficulties and a spirited resistance by the Britons, the Romans effected a landing, and once they had formed up on shore, easily routed the enemy. But as Caesar's cavalry had not been able to hold their course after him, the Romans being without horse could not pursue the Britons and complete their victory.[2]

But the Britons having now perceived with their own eyes that the tales of Roman invincibility which had reached them were only too true, immediately repented of their hostile attitude. As shortly before they had sent ambassadors to Caesar in Gaul, probably as an attempt to conciliate him and prevent his expedition to Britain, so now again they hastened to make their peace with him and agreed to submit to his authority.[3] Commius, who had been put in irons as the result of a popular revulsion of feeling against the overweening Roman who had sent him to announce his intention of immediately going in sovereign power to Britain, returned to Caesar with the new embassy of peace.[4] Caesar pardoned the tribes for breaking the promises made by their former embassy, but commanded them to deliver a number of hostages to him, disband their forces and go back to their homes. Part of the hostages were immediately handed over, while the chiefs

---

1. Caesar states the distance between Boulogne and his landing place in Britain to be about thirty miles (B.G. V. 2). Romney Marsh is the only place of disembarcation that satisfies the requirement of distance and the other conditions of tide and topography that appear in B. G. IV. 23 and V. 8-9. Here too was later Portus Lemanae, from which a Roman road ran to London. Here the Claudian armament landed in 43 A. D. (see ch. V). cp. also Caes. B. G. V. 11. where he says the Thames is eighty miles from the sea, that is from Romney. See Lewin's "Caesar's Invasions of Britain"; Malden in Journ. of Phil. XVII. 163-178, and XIX. 193-199. Their position on this point was not shaken by Ridgeway, J. of P. XIX.
2. B. G. IV. 26.   3. B. G. IV. 27. 1.
4. B. G. IV. 27. 2-4. cp. Rhys, Celtic Britain p. 62.

began to come from all quarters and commend themselves to Caesar.[1]

But two unforeseen mishaps soon befel the Romans, which restored confidence to the Britons and placed the Romans in great danger. The eighteen vessels with the cavalry on board were borne down the channel past the camp at Romney by a furious storm, and finally all returned to the continent. This same storm combined with the spring tide, a new thing to the Romans, to wreck many of Caesar's vessels on the beach at Romney. The Roman army was thrown almost into a panic, because they saw their means of retreat to the continent destroyed and had brought no provisions for a long stay in Britain.[2]

Seeing that the British chiefs encouraged by these things were concocting a conspiracy against him, Caesar resolved to forestall them by first breaking the peace himself. Accordingly, he sent part of his men into the fields of ripe grain to seize provision for the camp, while the rest kept watch over the intrenchments and repaired most of the damaged ships with materials from twelve which were hopelessly ruined.[3] Meanwhile the British forces gathered and waiting for a good opportunity, fell upon the seventh legion one day as it was engaged in reaping grain. A hot conflict ensued, in which the Romans succeeded in beating off their assailants only after the timely arrival of Caesar with reinforcements from the camp. They then made good their retreat to the camp, being without cavalry with which to follow up their advantage.[4]

The Britons now perceived that the Romans without cavalry and unfamiliar with the strange style of fighting which they had to face, were not eager to resume the offensive.[5] Elated at the hesitation and

---

1. IV. 27. 5-7.   2. IV. 28-30.   3. B. G. IV. 31.   4. IV. 34. 1-2.
5. IV. 34. 2.

helplessness of their enemy, the chieftains prepared for a grand concerted attack on the Roman camp. They hoped to annihilate this foreign force and so deter the masters of the continent from any future invasion of their island.[1] Foot and horse assembled from all quarters. The attack was made on the Roman camp, but resulted in a failure. The Britons could not long withstand the onset of the Roman infantry. While they could not turn their victory to account by a pursuit, the legions nevertheless ravaged some of the country roundabout on foot, and then returned to their camp by the shore.[2]

Again the Britons resorted to negotiations. Their peace emissaries were welcome enough to Caesar, who was glad of any excuse to retire from his difficult position unmolested. He therefore accepted their offers of peace, but being anxious to get back to Gaul without delay, he ordered the hostages that he demanded, twice as many as before, to be sent to him on the continent. The same night, after a stay of three weeks in Britain, he embarked his men and sailed for the coast of Gaul, where all the vessels arrived in safety.[3]

In this first expedition the Romans added little to their military prestige. A force without cavalry and impedimenta was not likely to impress the barbarians very deeply. If the cavalry had not failed him, Caesar would have made a good showing against the Britons, in spite of the shortness of time at his disposal.[4] As it was, he did not penetrate the country beyond the coast, but remained the whole three weeks close to his camp.[5] Still, the real objects of this tentative expedition were in the main attained. Caesar learnt what sort of vessels was required for his purposes, and ascertained

---
1. IV. 34. 5; IV. 30. 2.   2. IV. 35.   3. IV. 36.
4. Cp. the rapidity of his movements in the second campaign, V. 15 ff.
5. Cp. V. 9. 8, loci naturam ignorabat. The "place" was near the shore.

the nature of the landing-place, the British style of warfare and something of their character.

During the winter Caesar's legates saw to the building of a great fleet for a second invasion of Britain. Caesar had intended two expeditions from the beginning, the first being merely to prepare the way for the second.[1] He was, moreover, not at all satisfied with his first expedition, which not only left a poor impression upon the islanders and so failed of its political object, but was likely to be ridiculed by his enemies at Rome, as it was.[2] His reputation as a general needed to be vindicated. Besides nothing had yet been established as to the resources and geography of Britain. This discovery of a "new world," as Caesar himself called it,[3] served only to stimulate Roman curiosity. Caesar's official letter to the senate containing a detailed report of his actions, called forth a decree for a twenty days' public thanksgiving to the gods.[4] Dio says, with some exaggeration, that the people at home had now seen Caesar actually reach lands which were not even heard of before, and were so sanguine as to think already their own what existed as yet only in their hopes.[5] Everybody was talking about Britain, and not only its supposed wealth,[6] but the peculiar character of its people, their war-paint and their war-chariots were common topics of discussion.[7] Private enterprise fitted out more than one hundred vessels which accompanied Caesar's fleet in his second expedition, and would have been only the advance guard of many more had Britain proved worth exploiting.[8]

By the summer of 54 B. C. about six hundred

---

1. IV. 20. 2.   2. Lucan II. 572.
3. Eumen. Paneg. Constant. Caes. ch. XI.
4. B. G. IV. 38.   5. XXXIX. 53.
6. Cic. ad Fam. VII. 7.   7. Cic. ad Fam. VII. 6.
8. B. G. V. 2. Caesar had already his doubts about British wealth (cp. Cic. ad Att. IV. 16).

new vessels, built on the lines dictated to Caesar by the previous year's experience, were ready. These and twenty-eight battleships Caesar ordered to rendezvous at Portus Itius. All arrived except sixty, which were prevented by contrary winds. Four thousand Gallic cavalry and the leading men of all the states also came to Portus Itius. This time Caesar intended to make sure of quiet in Gaul during his absence by carrying along with him as hostages all the state leaders except a very few whose loyalty he could trust.[1] While his first expedition had been confessedly only a reconnoitre of a few weeks, this second might result in the permanent occupation of territories in Britain. Therefore Caesar took with him a far stronger force than before, and impedimenta and stores suitable for a prolonged stay.[2] He was prepared if necessary to remain in Britain during the winter.[3]

Only two of all the British tribes that had engaged to send hostages to Caesar in Gaul kept their promise.[4] But more useful than hostages was the arrival of young Mandubracius, the son of the ex-king of the Trinovantes, one of the strongest tribes in south-east Britain, taking refuge with Caesar from the pursuit of Cassivelaunus, who had dethroned and murdered his father. Mandubracius went along with Caesar to Britain eager to be revenged on Cassivelaunus with Roman help.[5] By restoring him to his rightful kingdom and upholding the cause of the Trinovantes against the encroachments of the Catuelauni, of whom Cassivelaunus seems to have been king,[6] Caesar saw

---

1. V. 5.

2. The number of the vessels shows that the impedimenta must have been very considerable.

3. B. G. V. 8. Labieno relicto ut portus tueretur et re frumentariae provideret, quaeque in Gallia gererentur cognosceret consiliumque pro tempore et pro re caperet. Cp. V. 22. 4 ; Cic. ad Q. F. III. 3. 4.

4. IV. 38.   5. V. 20.

6. Rhys, Celtic Britain, p. 15.

that he would obtain a basis for Roman dominion in Britain like the Ubii in Germany and the Haedui in Gaul.

Having completed all his arrangements, Caesar left Labienus in command of three legions and two thousand cavalry, with plenary powers to direct Gallic affairs during his absence, and himself took five legions with two thousand cavalry.[1] He sailed at midnight, about the 6th of July,[2] with more than eight hundred vessels altogether, of which over one hundred were private outfits. When the Britons saw them coming, they fled in terror into the woods, afraid to offer any resistance to such a huge armament.[3] Caesar had therefore no trouble this time in landing his troops and pitching a great camp on a favorable site.[4]

Meanwhile the British forces retreated northward about twelve miles from the sea, where they made a stand in a very strong position. But the Romans easily stormed their log fortress and chased them into the woods beyond. Further pursuit however was delayed for ten days, because of a storm which made havoc among the vessels on the beach.[5] But after the fleet had been repaired by strenuous exertions, at a loss of forty vessels, and orders had been sent to Labienus for more ships, as many as he could furnish, Caesar again gave the word to advance.[6]

In the preceding summer the Romans had but touched the shore of Britain and met probably none but the Belgian and Cantian tribes.[7] This year Caesar had formed a definite plan of operations. His aim was

---

1. V. 8.
2. Real time July 6th, i. e. July 30th of pre-Julian calendar. See Vogel in Jahrbb. fur classische Philol. (1890), p. 276.
3. B. G. V. 8.
4. Dio, XL. 1.3, correctly infers from Caes. V. 8. 3 that Caesar landed in the same place as in 55 B. C.
5. Caes. V. 10 cp. Cic. ad Q. F. III. 1. 13.
6. B. G. V. 11.   7. See next chapter.

to penetrate straightway to the territories of the Trinovantes in Essex county, and there establish his base of operations with the support of Mandubracius and his people. The Britons made use of Caesar's enforced delay to spread the alarm in all directions and rally their countrymen in a common cause against the foreign invader. Cassivelaunus, now the most powerful prince in Britain, perfectly aware of Caesar's designs against him, took the command of the national army.[1] Fighting went on for a few days in Kent. But though the Britons showed great cunning and a remarkable quickness to take advantage of the embarrassment of their enemy in a difficult and unknown country, and even won some successes in infantry engagements,[2] they were as chaff before the wind in a close encounter with their disciplined opponents. After a severe reverse the native army melted away, and Cassivelaunus could not again succeed in mustering a united opposition to Caesar's movements.[3] The Romans now advanced with ease to the Thames, which they crossed about August 6th,[4] probably at Coway Stakes near Kingston. Led by Mandubracius, he pushed on through a wooded district, harassed on all sides by the guerrilla tactics of Cassivelaunus, who had now ascertained the folly of attempting to meet his enemy in the open, towards the Trinovantes. He had not long to wait before their ambassadors came to meet him and offer obedience to Rome if only he would free them from the yoke of their old enemies, the Catuelauni, and restore to them Mandubracius.[5]

Caesar, complying with their request, installed Mandubracius and ordered forty hostages and corn

1. B. G. V. 11. 9.
2. Dio XL. 3 cp. Tac. Agr. 12, in pedite robur.
3. B. G. V. 17. 5.
4. See Vogel 1. c. pp. 280, 287. He cites Cic. ad Q. F. III. 1. 25.
5. B. G. V. 20.

for his army. These commands being fulfilled with alacrity, he proceeded to treat the Trinovantes as friends of the Roman People.[1]

When the other tribes, many of them tributary to Cassivelaunus, saw that the Trinovantes were now exempt from the ravages and plunder of the Romans, and were also rid of Cassivelaunus and his tyranny, they hastened likewise to surrender to Caesar. Stripped of his allies and dependents, Cassivelaunus retreated to his stronghold, probably near the modern St. Albans,[2] hidden away in the heart of swamps and thick woods. But Caesar's new allies, eager to show themselves serviceable to him and to settle old scores with Cassivelaunus, guided the Romans to the place which was not far away.[3] The Catuelauni did not long abide the assault of the legions, but abandoned the fort and their large herds of cattle and fled into the forest.[4]

Meanwhile as a last attempt to stave off surrender, Cassivelaunus had sent orders to four Cantian kings to mobilize their whole force, surprise the Roman camp on the shore, and so by a sudden stroke destroy Caesar's means of retreat from the island. But the Roman guard easily repulsed the attack of the Cantians, and Caesar's connections with the camp, for a time imperilled by this movement in his rear, were restored.[5] Hearing of this final failure and disheartened by his losses, the ravages of his territory and, most of all, the defection of his allies, Cassivelaunus confessed himself beaten and begged for peace.

Caesar was glad to end the war so soon, for the latest news from Gaul had decided him to winter on the continent.[6] Besides it is probable that he found it

1. B. G. V. 21. 1.
2. See Arch. Journ. XXII. p. 229.
3. V. 21. 2.   4. V. 21. 5.
5. V. 22, cp. Vogel l. c. pp. 280-282, 287. He cites Cic. ad Q. F. III. 3. 1, etc.
6. V. 22 ; Dio XL. 4; Strabo IV. 5. 3.

difficult to provision his army.[1] But the chief reason for Caesar's speedy withdrawal from Britain, one which he wisely does not mention in the commentaries, was beyond a doubt the conviction that there was nothing to be gained from the island, and that it would never pay for its conquest. Further fighting would only be wasting his time and his men. Caesar therefore lost no time in granting terms of peace. He ordered hostages to be immediately delivered, fixed an annual tribute which Britain should pay to Rome, and commanded Cassivelaunus not to disturb Mandubracius in his kingdom.[2]

The hostages received, Caesar marched back to the sea about the beginning of September, with a great number of captives but very little other booty.[3] It was close upon the equinox when he shook the dust of Britain from his feet, packed his last men into the boats and scudded away from the rainy land of savages and forests to the land of his adoption, where many men in after times were to bear the name of Julius.[4] And the Britons who watched from the rocks and dunes the eager haste of the departing conquerors and saw not a soldier left behind to hold them to their allegiance,[5] must soon have persuaded themselves that while they minded their own affairs and did not interfere in any way with Roman interests on the continent, it would be long before Roman arms would again seek glory in their poor, uninviting island.

The second expedition, while highly successful from a military point of view, had proved that Britain was no easy prize for the Roman capitalist. There were no rich mines of gold or silver or diamonds or fabled electrum in this wild northern land. Nor could

---

1. Cp. B. G. VI. 29. 1.   2. V. 22.
3. B. G. V. 23. 2.   Plutarch, Caes. 23.   Cic. ad Att. IV. 18.   See Vogel l. c. p. 284.   4. V. 23. 5.   5. Dio XL. 4.

the inhabitants appreciate the wares of civilization.[1] The enterprising merchants who sent out over a hundred vessels with Caesar must have been greatly disappointed. At that time Britain's available wealth lay not in mines but in cattle and furs, and this was not the kind of wealth that Roman capital could turn to best account. Slave labor on a great scale could never become profitable so far north. Besides, the Italian shuddered at the thought of British skies and chilly swamps.[2] Caesar therefore made no effort to retain possession of Britain. He had made his discoveries, hardened his soldiers, increased his military fame and demonstrated Roman invincibility to the uttermost barbarians.[3] But beyond the glory of the expedition and its scientific value, it was made evident that no material gain was likely to accrue to the Roman empire from an annexation of Britain.[4] Perhaps Caesar afterwards thought at times of a conquest of Britain in the far future. There he saw good material for the imperial armies, and great agricultural possibilities. But there was plenty of good soldiers nearer the Rhine and as for agriculture, the Roman "latifundia" would never find a congenial home in Britain.

No danger threatened the peace of the empire from Britain.[5] But the north of Italy lay wide open to the tribes of Germany. The principal object of Augustus' foreign policy was to secure tranquillity for Italy by pushing forward Roman rule north and east of the Alps, and east of Gaul. Thus not only was a bulwark raised against the northern tribes, but it was attempted to shorten the frontier line of the empire by

---

[1]. William Vernon Harcourt says that "England has no great trade interests at stake in countries where the people do not wear clothes." The same was true of Rome.
[2]. Tac. Agr. 12 : coelum imbribus foedum. Cp. Germ. 2.
[3]. Cp. Froude, Caesar, p. 288.   [4]. See Strabo II. 5. 8.
[5]. Strabo II. 5. 8. Tac. Ann. II. 24.

the annexation of Germany to the Elbe and, at the same time, to remove farther from the imperial capital the great masses of the standing army.[1] While this important scheme was on the tapis, it is no wonder that Britain was left to herself.

1. Schiller I. 214.

CHAPTER III.

THE BRITONS.

At the time of Caesar's invasion the British tribes differed widely among themselves in physical aspect, customs, language, religion and some little in political organization.[1] The Gaelic tribes of Cornwall and Devon, part of Wales, northern Scotland, and Ireland were distinguished by red hair and a more ferocious appearance from the yellow-haired Brythons who had dispossessed them of most of England and southern Scotland.[2] Having been the first to break off from the Celtic stock on the continent, the Gaels or Goidels preserved in their island home the wild barbarism common to the old Celts and the Germans.[3] On the continent the Celts had made progress towards civilization, leaving far behind them in some respects their Teutonic neighbors.[4] But among the Gaels the old patriarchal kings continued to hold sway.[5] Their religious or magic rites, paralleled in savage horrors only by the Teutonic sacrifices to Woden and Thor, flourished down to the time of Pliny the Elder.[6] These people appear to have had little or no knowledge of agriculture, no coinage and scarcely any skill in manufacture.[7]

The civilization of the Brythonic tribes varied according to the time of their departure from the

---

1. Tac. Agr. 11. Mela III. 51. Rhys, Celtic Britain ch. I.
2. Elton, Origins of Eng. Hist. p. 158. Tac. Agr. 24, says the Hibernians differed little from the Britons—that is from the Gaelic Britons. Solinus and other authors mention the ferocity of the Hibernians.
3. Herodian III. 14. Dio LXXVI. 12.
4. Caes. VI. 12; VI. 24.
5. Diodor. Sic. V. 21. Tac. Agr. 24. cp. Tac. Germ. 7, for the Germans.
6. H. N. XXX. 4.
7. Mela III. 51. Caes. V. 14. Strabo IV. 5. 4. Solinus 22. cp. Tac. Germ. 5, for the Germans.

continent. The oldest arrivals, the Brigantes of northern England, the Catuelauni whose princes had established their rule over most of central England, the Iceni of Norfolk and Suffolk, and the Trinovantes of Essex were up to Caesar's invasion probably little more advanced than the Gaels.[1] The Belgic tribes south of the Thames, the Atrebates, Belgae, etc., who had not long before Caesar's time crossed from the mainland,[2] and the Cantii of Kent who were the least uncivilized of all the Britons through their slight intercourse with Gallic merchants,[3] resembled closely the Belgic Gauls opposite them on the continent.[4] But even the Cantii and the Belgae had been, as was natural, partially assimilated to the more barbarous inhabitants of the interior. While they practised agriculture with considerable skill,[5] dressed very like the Gauls,[6] and lived in huts like those of the mainland,[7] they all dyed themselves with woad,[8] took the savage's delight in gaudy trinkets[9] and used the same tactics in war as the other Britons. Unlike their continental cousins they still continued, like their northern neighbors, to be governed by kings,[10] though the power of some of the kings, like that of the German princes, must have been rather patriarchal in its nature; certainly not despotic, but quite limited by popular rights.[11] Other tribal kings there were, however, who got a firmer power through their ruling a subject, non-Aryan race.

The language of the Brythons and Belgic Gauls must have been somewhat the same. The Gaels on the other hand spoke an altogether different dialect of Celtic.[12]

1. Caes. V. 14.
2. Caes. II. 4. 7. Perhaps however the time was much earlier than "nostra memoria" would seem to imply. Barbarians could not give Caesar very exact chronological information.   3. V. 14.   4. Tac. Agr. 11.   5. Elton, p. 119.
6. Elton, p. 114.   7. Caes. V. 12.   8. V. 14.   9. Strabo IV. 5.
10. V. 22. Cp. Diodor. Sic. V. 21 ; Tac. Ann. II. 24.
11. Caes. IV. 27. 4.   Cp. Holder, Germ. Altertumer note on Tac. Germ. 7.
12. Rhys, C. B. ch. I. See Tac. Germ. 45.

One more nationality in Britain attracted the attention of the ancient writers by its utter contrast to the Celtic tribes. The Silures of southern Wales were a race of short, dusky men with black, curly hair, according to Tacitus like the Iberians of Spain.[1] He was puzzled to account for their presence among the tall, blonde Celts in this western corner of the island. Probably the remnant of a non-Aryan race which dwelt in Britain before the Celtic invasion, mingled to some extent with the Gaels,[2] the Silures held tightly together, rejecting the devices of civilization,[3] and by their dogged valor long stood their ground against both Brythons and Romans.[4]

On the whole, it may be regarded as fairly certain that the British tribes, though originally of the same race as the Gauls and speaking various dialects of Celtic, were in their political and social condition nearer to the Teutons than to the semi-civilized Celts of Gaul. The British tribes, as has been said, were still under patriarchal kings, or cantonal princes,[5] who probably in many cases exercised the triple function of general, judge and high-priest.[6] As in Germany, so in Britain there had developed a strong tendency to the union of several clans under one powerful chief. The confederacy of the Suebi is paralleled by the ascendency of the Catuelaunian princes, Cassivelaunus, Cunobellinus and Caratacus, by the Brigantian state and by the union of Caledonian tribes under Calgacus. The growth of an embittered opposition to these aggrandizing powers by confederacies of lesser tribes in Germany and Britain[7] invited the intervention of Rome in the affairs of those countries. Having already entered upon a decline in

---

1. Tac. Agr. 11.   Elton, ch. VI.
2. Elton, ch. VI.   Rhys, pp. 80, 215.
3. Solinus 22.   4. Tac. Ann. XII. 32.
5. Tac. Ann. II. 24: "remissi a *regulis.*"
6. Perhaps called "druid" sometimes.   7. B. G. V. 11, 9.

vigor and warlike spirit,[1] the mass of the Gauls fell quickly before Roman force and culture. But the love of freedom and loyalty to their own rude institutions still inspired the Germans and the British Celts to make great sacrifices for their independence. The Britons were not cowards on foot like their Gallic kinsmen.[2] Their strength, says Tacitus, lay in their infantry.[3] Dio Cassius also alludes to the fighting qualities of the British foot.[4] But like the Germans, even this brave people could not stand before the Roman legion in the open field.

The religion of the ancient Britons must have resembled very closely that of the Germans and the old Celts, though it is difficult, owing to the lack of explicit information on the subject by Roman and Greek writers, to state anything in regard to details with certainty. While in Gaul the Celts had in their progress towards civilization evolved a distinct learned class of bards, priests, and philosopher-magicians called Druids, "Very Wise Ones,"[5] who exercised a great power among the people,[6] it is more than probable that in Britain, as in Germany, the priests or magicians had not attained to such political pre-eminence. The Gaulish Druids had acquired a power comparable to that of the Brahmins in India. They constituted a privileged class quite fenced off from the common herd of serfs whom they spurned and cheated.[7] But there is no evidence of the existence of such an independent hierarchy in Britain. There, it would appear, the popular religion, the elastic polytheism of all the Aryans,[8] had retained its old forms,

1. B. G. VI. 24. cp. Froude, Caes. p. 216.
2. Cp. Froude, p. 296-7. Momm. Hist. IV. 277-8.
3. Agr. 12. cp. Germ. 6, for the Germans.
4. XL. 3.   5. Holder, Altkeltischer Sprachschatz.
6. Diodor. Sic. V. 31. Strabo IV. 4. 4.   7. Caes. VI. 13, 14.
8. Rhys, C. B. p. 67. cp p. 99—"There is no evidence that Druidism was ever the religion of any Brythonic people." Much less therefore had the less civilized Gaels developed such a hierarchy. See p. 36, n. 4.

primitive and hearty, though doubtless in some respects very cruel and bloody. It would appear that the British priest or magician, though pretending to none of the metaphysical or cosmogonic knowledge which the Gallic Druids claimed to have gained, nor belonging to an organized hierarchy under an arch-priest,[1] yet exercised like the Teutonic priests[2] a great power over the individuals of his canton. Frequently the chief and the high priest of a British clan or sept must have been one and the same person. It is possible that the Britons with their Celtic proneness to superstitious fears, were more devoted to magic rites, sacrifices and incantations than the Germans.[3] But the silence of ancient writers about a British hierarchy, and Caesar's express denial of the existence of such an organization in Germany[4] must lead to the conclusion that neither in Britain nor in Germany was there anything approaching a close corporation of priests with large political powers.

Solinus speaking of the Silures[5] says that among them men and women alike prophesied about the future. In Britain therefore as in Germany,[6] women played an important part in the interpretation of the supernatural. The British medicine-men or medicine-women, any who might possess superior intelligence or cunning, and likewise the power of beguiling themselves and others by a rude eloquence, were as far removed from the Gallic Druids as the despised private augurs at Rome from the stately college of augurs recognized as a political institution.

But the best evidence against a supposition that the British priests whether clan leaders or ordinary

---

1. Caes. VI. 13. 8.   2. Holder, on Tac. Germ. 7.
3. Cp. Pliny XXX. 4 with Caes. VI. 21. But see also Tac. Germ. 10, "Franci divinationibus dediti."   4. Caes. VI. 21.
5. Ch. 22. Cp. perhaps Mela III. 48.   6. Tac. Germ. 8.

medicine-men, were organized like the Gallic Druids as
a powerful caste[1] extending its influence far beyond
the limits of tribe or state, and fostering a national
religious union, is the fact that no ancient writer
so much as hints at any priest-directed, national religious
movement among the Britons against Roman rule.[2]
Political and economic considerations, and not religious
feeling, are assigned by Tacitus and Dio to the British
revolt of 61 A. D.[3] The British and German priests or
seers were at best the counterpart of the Gallic *Iliereis*
described by Strabo and Diodorus Siculus, rather than
of the Druids who were regularly graduated theologians
and altogether loftier in aspirations and ideas than the
priests of the savage, skin-clad Britons could have been.

But it has been commonly asserted that Druidism
was a vast system of religion with an organized priesthood which had its origin and high seat in Britain,
whence it spread to the Celts of Gaul and Spain.[4] One
writer voices well the prevailing belief when he says:
"In the corporation of the Druids the Celtic nation
though politically extremely divided had its centre and
preserved a strong national consciousness."[5] Some of the
bolder spirits, flinging caution to the winds, pronounce
the island of Mona (Anglesey) to have been "the chief
seat of the priestly system" of the whole Celtic race,[6]
"the true focus of the national and religious resistance,"[7] and "the centre of the Celtic agitation."[8]

It is somewhat difficult to accept this theory of the
existence in Britain of a mighty order of Druids of
which that in Gaul was but a pale reflection. It is perhaps still harder to conceive of Mona as the grand

1. Cp. Auson. (Peiper's Edition pp. 52, 59) "stirpe druidarum."
2. The contrary in Gaul. See Tac. Hist. IV. 54.
3. Ann. XIV. 31; Agr. 15. Dio LXII. 2 *ff*.
4. Mommsen, Prov. I. 188 *ff*. Ranke, Huebner, and others.
5. Paul: Das Druidentum, Fleckeisens Jahrbucher, Vol. 145 (1892) p. 769-797.
6. Mommsen, Prov. I. p. 188.   7. Mommsen, Prov. I. p. 193.
8. Jung, p. 280.

shrine, the Mecca of the Celtic race, without further evidence than the assertions of modern historians. The foundation for the fabric of legend, dream and rhetoric which has been erected and inscribed with the name of British Druidism seems to be a very free misinterpretation of a passage in Caesar, and one in Tacitus, helped out by some false philology. Caesar mentions in his brief account of Druidism some story about a British origin for the doctrines and ritual of the order.[1] But it has already been shown how Caesar was deceived,[2] and indeed the theory of a British origin for Druidism is now generally discredited.[3]

Caesar found no Druidism in Britain or he would surely have at least mentioned it as supporting the legend which he found among the Gallic Druids ascribing a British origin to their order. Yet the tribes which Caesar visited were just the ones that had been in a position to receive and transmit a spreading religion either from Gaul to Britain or from Britain to Gaul.[4] Apparently Caesar had himself little faith in the tradition.[5]

The other classical authority, so-called, for the existence of the Druidic system in Britain is Tacitus. In relating the expedition of Suetonius Paulinus to the island of Mona, he says that Mona was populous and a refuge for fugitives, but neglects to note in this connection that Mona was "the focus of the national and religious resistance." Then follows an interesting chapter describing the reception that was arranged for

[1]. B. G. VI. 13.   [2]. Ch. 1.
[3]. Deservedly, for the Britons had scarcely any intercourse with the mainland and what they had was only passive. Surely they sent no missionaries there. Cp. Rhys, C. B. p. 72.
[4]. It was the Cantii who had intercourse with Gaul, not the Dumnonii or Silures (Caes. V. 14. 1).
[5]. If Gauls studied in Britain, it is strange that Caesar did not apply to some of them, in 55 B. C., for information about the island. But evidently the Gauls did not go to Britain to study in the fogs and swamps of Siluria.

the Romans on the shore of the island, a great demonstration by "Druids praying and cursing, and women running about dressed in funereal black,[1] with torches in their hands and hair wildly flowing." But the Romans after a brief spell of consternation and dismay overcame their fears and easily quelled " a mob of fanatics and women." Then the sacred groves, oaks no doubt, were cut down and the altars defiled with human gore broken in pieces.[2]

Even if this passage of the text be sound, its strong rhetorical flavor, the suddenness with which the Druids are introduced and also dropped, and the reminiscent quality of certain features tell against its historical value. In the "women dressed in funereal black, looking like the Furies," there is a damning echo of Strabo's account of the Iberian Cassiterides,[3] especially significant as Tacitus and others connected the Silures with the Iberians. The sentence nam —— cruore habebant is a bald paraphrase from a passage in Diodorus Siculus (V. 31), and quite unworthy of Tacitus. The cutting down of the sacred trees by a soldiery which hesitated at first recalls the unwillingness of Caesar's men to cut down the oaks at Massilia.[4] It would appear therefore that the writer of this chapter, understanding that Mona was a sacred island of the western Britons, and remembering the stories of old authors about divine or haunted islands in the Atlantic Ocean, grafted their descriptions in part upon Mona, with added touches

---

1. The black appears to be an error in detail, so far as Druidism is concerned (see Pelloutier, Hist. des Celtes II. 312, and Pliny, H. N. XVI. 95). But the writer follows Strabo, neck or nothing.   2. Ann. XIV. 30.

3. Strabo III. 5. 11, who quotes from some earlier romancer. Cp. also IV. 4. 6, cited above, page 9, n. 2. Putting these two passages together, Tacitus or whoever wrote this flaming rhetoric on Mona (Ann. XIV. 30), was able to draw quite a grand picture of a mock-supernatural scene. With the whole account cp. Plutarch, De Def. Orac. 18, and for the sacred island cp. Tac. Germ. 40.

4. Lucan III. 429 *ff.*

derived from a confused identification of British priests and rites with those of Gaul.[1]

But it seems probable that Tacitus did not write all at any rate of this chapter. Nowhere does he allude to Druidism as a religious system of Britain. In the eleventh chapter of his Life of Agricola, he says that the Britons nearest to Gaul, that is the Belgae and Cantii, had the same religion and superstitions as the Gauls[2]—that is, the Belgic Gauls.[3] But Druidism had little or no hold upon the Belgic Gauls.[4] The Belgae plumed themselves upon their German origin and customs. The most civilized of the Britons were therefore much nearer to the Germans in manner of life and institutions than to the Gauls proper.

If Mona had been a centre of Druidism or any other religion, one would certainly expect some indication of it at the end of Tac. Agr. 14. An attack on a national sanctuary would have called for some reference to it in Agr. 15, where the causes of the British uprising are set forth. But Tacitus does not suggest that the disaffected Britons were "exasperated by Paulinus' attack on the most sacred seat of the national religion," or that "the old vehement Celtic faith burst forth for the last time."[5] He simply says that the Britons discounted their fear of Rome "in the absence of the legate," who by going to so distant a place as

---

1. Even a half intelligent writer could have been misled by the fact that the word druid was common to the Gallic and British languages, though with far different content.

2. Tac. Agr. 11. Caes. V. 14. Just as he thought the Iberians of Spain had occupied the west part of Britain, so Tacitus believed that the Gauls had possessed themselves of the south-east part.

3. Cp. Caes V. 12. 2 and II. 4. 7 with I. 1. 2. It was the Belgae who had occupied south-east Britain, and they were very different from the other Gauls.

4. Caes. VI. 13 does not include the Belgae "in omni Gallia." Cp. VI. 12, where the Haedui and Sequani are called the leading states of Gaul. They certainly did not lord it over the Belgae—cp. B. G. I. 1. Caesar generally excludes the Belgae from Gaul. See II. 3, II. 4, VI. 24, and cp. I. 1. 6, I. 30. He says distinctly (I. 1. 2) that the institutions of Gaul proper and Belgica differ. Cp. p. 33 n. 8 and Froude, Caes. p. 216.   5. Mommsen. Prov. I. 195.

Mona, gave them a chance to plot behind his back. When in the eleventh chapter of the Agricola Tacitus proposes an Iberian origin for the Silures, he beyond all doubt knows nothing of any Druidic religion among them. Otherwise he would most certainly have compared it with that of the Gauls proper, just as he compared the superstitions of the Belgic Britons to those of the Belgic Gauls.

In introducing the subject of Mona (Ann. XIV. 29), Tacitus does not mention that it was a sacred island. Then in the next chapter suddenly comes a vivid picture of Mona as a Druidical stronghold. Dio Cassius in describing the same events knows nothing of the Druids and altars of Mona. He simply tells how the revolt of the Britons took place while "Paulinus the governor was on an expedition to *a certain* island Mona situated close to Britain."[1] And Dio was not the man to miss any chance for a bit of lively writing, provided it were at all compatible with historical accuracy.[2] Moreover, Dio seems to have used the same sources as Tacitus for the reign of Nero, if not Tacitus himself.[3]

But perhaps the strongest evidence of all for believing that Tacitus is not responsible for the whole of this chapter (Ann. XIV. 30) is the statement that Suetonius Paulinus placed a garrison in Mona. This must be absolutely untrue, for the British insurrection which at this juncture arose in his rear, did not permit Paulinus to dispense with a man. He immediately abandoned Mona without waiting to complete its subjugation, and marched eastward with his whole force, small enough in the face of a general revolt.[4]

It seems therefore that this isolated passage, commonly accepted as proof of British Druidism, bears

1. Dio LXII. 7.
2. Cp. Haupt, Philologus (1885) p. 162, on Dio's accuracy.
3. Philol. (1885) pp. 145, 150, 161.
4. Tac. Ann. XIV. 31. Cp. Agr. 18.

upon its face ample cause for our rejecting it. The silence of ancient writers as to Druidism in Britain becomes more significant when contrasted with the mass of testimony which proves this system of religion to have been peculiar to Gaul. The following passages may serve as examples :—

> Cic.—De Divinatione I. 41 :—" In Gallia Druidae sunt."
>
> Strabo IV. 4. 4 describes Druidism in Gaul at some length.
>
> Diodor. Sic. V. 31 gives an account of Gallic Druids.
>
> Mela III. 2, III. 18—Account of Gallic Druids.
>
> Lucan I. 450 *ff* refers to the Druids of Gaul.
>
> Pliny H. N. XXIX. 12. 1 "Galliarum Druidae." XXIV. 62. 1 "Druidae Gallorum." XVI. 95. 1 "Galliarum admiratio * * * Druidae (ita suos appellant magos)," etc. XXX. 4 "Tiberius sustulit druidas Gallorum." Cp. the following paragraph, in which Pliny refers to the excessive superstitions of the Britons, comparing their practice of magic ("eam artem." i. e. magicam, "celebrat,") to that of Persia, not Gaul. The Druids, in Pliny's opinion, are a peculiarly Gallic order of magicians. To no others does he give a specific name.
>
> Tacitus Hist. IV. 54 shows how the centre at any rate of Druidism and of Druidic opposition to Rome was in Gaul. Cp. Pliny H. N. XXX. 4 and Sueton. Claud. 25. We never hear of a similar organized and organizing force in Britain.
>
> Suetonius, Claud. 25—"Druidarum religionem apud Gallos penitus abolevit." If Claudius invaded Britain, as is commonly asserted, in order to crush the national spirit of the Celts

in Gaul by striking a death-blow at the heart of the Druidic system in Britain, Suetonius seems to have been unaware of any such policy. If it had been so he would not have said only "apud Gallos."

Ammianus XV. 9—Account of the Druids of Gaul.

Origen, contra Celsum I. 16, mentions the Druids of the Gauls.

Diogenes Laertius, Proem. 4—"Among the Keltoi," i. e. Germans, etc., "and the Gauls the so-called Druids." Britons were of course not included among the Keltoi.

Clemens Alexandrinus, Stromata I. 15, in a list of the magi of the different nations, enumerates "the Prophets of the Egyptians, the Chaldees of Assyria, the Druids of the Gauls, and the philosophers of the Keltoi." Nothing is said of the Britons.

Suidas (a strong witness)—*Druidai para Galatais philosophoi kai semnotheoi.*

To these passages which refer Druidism distinctly to Gaul, the following should be added, in which as describing the institutions of the Britons, one would expect to find some notice of Druidism, if it existed.

Caesar, B. G. V. 12-14. Strabo IV. 5. 1-3. Diodorus Siculus V. 21, 22. Solinus, ch. 22. Solinus says of the Silures that they "deos percolunt." Though inclined to exaggeration and fond of the strange and marvelous, Solinus does not betray any suspicion he may have harbored that Druids existed in Britain. Apparently he never dreamed of such a thing.

Tacitus Agr. 10-12, says nothing of Druids in Britain.

Add to these Dio Cassius LXII. 7-8. He treats Mona as an ordinary, natural island. By his time the nearer islands of the Atlantic had ceased to be fair game for careless falsifiers and miracle-mongers. Man-eating, grass-eating, nakedness and polyandry were now attributed only to the most remote parts of the British islands, Thule, etc.[1] Even Mona had emerged from the shadow of fable. It was now too well known to weave fanciful stories about.[2] Or perhaps we should say it had not yet re-entered the shadow which hid it from the gaze of Tacitus' monkish interpolator.[3]

The single passage of the Annals, therefore, which is thought to prove the existence of a Druidic hierarchy in Britain, either shows culpable carelessness on the part of Tacitus, or far more probably has been padded by some subsequent writer. Possibly Tacitus wrote with some truth that Mona was a sort of holy place for the British tribes of the vicinity, like the island referred to in the fortieth chapter of his Germania. But the passage as a whole, especially the trite phrase "praesidium impositum," savors of the officious interpolator. Certainly it can not be regarded as proving that Mona was a religious centre even for the western tribes, far less for the British tribes in general.

For even should this chapter of Tacitus be accepted in its entirety as sober, veracious history, it does not allow us to infer that the British "Druids" mentioned, whatever they were, formed part of a hierarchy however geographically limited, like that of Gaul; it does not provide the most devout believer in British Druidism with a shadow of evidence for a national religious system among the ancient Britons, much less for any comprehensive Celtic religion centring in Britain.

1. Dio LXXVI. 12, etc.
2. See Pliny's ignorance about the nights of Mona, H. N. II. 77.
3. Cp. Freeman, Norman Conquest, I. 557-559.

That the Celts of Britain, Hibernia and Gaul had scarcely any intercourse with one another[1] and no feeling of a common nationality[2] is enough to reduce to an absurdity the theory of a pan-Celtic religious system. If the Romans had ever heard of a religious union among the Celts of the islands and the mainland, writers like Caesar, Pliny and Tacitus would most surely have called attention to a system so wonderful and far reaching. Those writers who described Britain as almost sundered from the rest of the world must have been painfully ignorant of the purpose nowadays so wilfully attributed to Claudius in making his expedition.[3] If Claudius did aim at the final destruction of Druidism by invading its stronghold in Britain, he left his educated subjects singularly in the dark as to what he really accomplished. But the truth is that Druidism did not exist in Britain, to beckon the Roman legions to marches beyond the sea. The British tribes appear like the Germans to have possessed no national religious system.

It may be objected that the Irish word drui (sorcerer) and the Welsh derwydd prove the existence of Druids in the British Isles in ancient times. The crazy legends of Ireland and Wales are full of accounts of the old Druids, their magic powers and their contests with Christian saints.

"Our traditions of the Scottish and Irish Druids are evidently derived from a time when Christianity had long been established."[4] It is probable, however, that there were men called " druids" in ancient Britain, but according to the meaning assigned by Holder to the word (Old Celtic druid, from dru-vid-s, very wise),[5] they need not have been more than any wise or clever men. Very likely however the name "druid" was so far

---
1. See ch. I.   2. See ch. IV.   3 See next chapter.
4. Prof. O'Curry, quoted in Bonwick's Irish Druids p. 11.
5. Altkeltischer Sprachschatz.

specialized by the Britons as to be frequently applied *par excellence* to the priest or magus, who as among the Teutons[1] was invested with considerable powers, but possessed nothing like the peculiar rank and authority of the Gallic Druid. The word druid did not connote at all the same thing in Britain as in Gaul. In Gaul the Druid was a member of a not merely cantonal or tribal, but a national religious organization. There is not a jot of evidence for, but much against the existence of a priestly caste in the savage tribes of Britain. Like the Germans they seem to have made no such doubtful progress. While they may have had their druids, they had no Druidism in the proper sense of the word.[2]

If "Druidism" meant simply the early naturalistic religion of the Aryan tribes, the Britons would appear to have as good a claim to it as the Germans and Scandinavians, and no better. Louis de Baecker, in fact, holds that Druidism was the religion of the Germans and Scandinavians. One might as well declare at once that Romulus and Remus were under the spiritual guidance of Druids. But Druidism does not mean simply that naturalistic religion. As known to Latin and Greek writers, Druidism was the peculiar hierarchical religion of Gaul, and in this Britain or Germany had no part.

From the material condition alone of the Britons one would naturally infer that their religion was of the same general character as that of the Teutons. Few British tribes practised agriculture,[3] and many knew nothing of money.[4] All the Britons that Caesar saw dyed themselves with woad. The poets often allude to the painting and tattooing practised by British and German

1. Cp. Tac. Germ. 6, 7, 10, 11, 43, and see commentary in Holder's edition, p. 163 and pp. 185-189.
2. Cp. Dr. Richey quoted by Bonwick, p. 36: "The early Irish missionaries found no priesthood occupying a definite political position."
3. Caes. V. 14.   4. Caes. V. 12 and Solinus 22.

tribes.1 It is not surprising therefore to learn that the Britons like the Germans and even the Gauls were addicted to human sacrifices and other nefarious rites. The same naturalistic religion held sway among all the Celts and Germans.2 The oak-tree and the mistletoe were universally connected with superstitious beliefs.3 The night being held sacred as the mother of day, time was counted by nights.4 The abstention of some British tribes from the flesh of hare, chicken and goose is not paralleled among the Celts of Gaul.

In habits, dress and general life the Britons resembled the Germans closely. Long after the time of the Romans in Britain, Aneurin (Gododin, st. 90) writes of the British chieftain rejoicing in a coat of the speckled skins of young wolves. Only the coast tribes of the south-east seem to have clothed themselves in woven fabrics at the time of Caesar.5 The Britons had the same regard as the continental Celts for gay decorations. They delighted in tartans, beads, chains and rings.6 Like the Germans, the Britons were taller and more terrible to look upon than the Gauls.7

British manufactures had hardly outgrown infancy. There are some traces of pre-Roman weapons, glass beads, etc., made in Britain. Some of the southern tribes struck rude gold coins on the model of those circulating in Gaul.8 The tribes of the south-west seem to have mined tin and lead in a small way. Iron mining was developed only after Caesar's invasions to any extent.9 When later the Romans took possession of

1. E. g. Hor. Epod. XVI. 7 for the Germans.
2. Cp. Tac. Agr. 11 " superstitionum persuasiones."
3. See Wagler in Berliner Studien f. class. Phil. Vol. XIII. pp. 39-43.
4. Caes. VI. 18. cp. Eng. fortnight.   5. Cp. Caes. VI. 21 on the Germans.
6. Strabo IV. 5.   Dio LXII. 2.   Elton, ch. 5.
7. Strabo IV. 5. 2. Tac. Agr. 11. Caes. V. 14 " horridi in pugna." The Gauls were themselves very tall and strong—see Napoleon, Caes. 11. 36.
8. See Evans, Ancient Brit. Coinage.
9. Cp. Caes. V. 12 with Strabo IV. 5. 2.

the land, they kept the Britons at work in the old lead mines under more scientific direction.

Like the Germans the Britons lived in open villages.[1] The tendency to congregate in cities, already apparent in Gaul, was probably represented in Britain only in the case of London, which must have been the centre for what trade passed up and down the Thames.[2] After Caesar's departure from Britain, London became the emporium of a largely increased commerce with the continent. In the time of Strabo the products of Britain, corn, cattle, gold, silver and iron, as well as skins, hunting-dogs and slaves were eagerly sought by continental traders in exchange for ivory, chains, glass vessels and various trumpery.[3]

The powerful state of the Catuelauni under its kings Tasciovanus and Cunobellinus, who owned London, outstripped far the other tribes in this civilizing intercourse with the mainland.[4] Here were struck the finest of the British coins of this period. The reign of Cunobellinus was almost a golden age for the Catuelauni. The influence of growing civilization upon southeastern Britain is shown by the Latin legends on the coins of various states.

The population of southeastern Britain is described by Caesar as very dense, dwelling in huts close together. Perhaps we may say it was nearly as dense as that of Belgica, which has been estimated with wide exaggeration at two hundred to the square mile.[5]

---

1. Cp. Tac. Germ. 16.
2. That London was an important town before Roman times is shown by the failure of the Roman attempt to change its Celtic name. See Loftie, London (Hist. Towns Series) p. 2. For cities in Gaul see Mommsen, Hist. IV. 266.
3. Strabo IV. 5, 2. Note that Strabo does not include tin among the exports of Britain. cp. page 6 above, n. 2.
4. Sueton. Calig. 44 " rex Britannorum."
5. Mommsen, Hist. IV. 264. cp. Beloch, Bevolkerung der griechisch—romischen Welt pp. 448-460, who seems to underrate considerably the density. See also Richards in " Social England," I. p. 95.

The women of Britain, like those of Germany, seem to have held a higher position than the women of Gaul.[1] In social life as in everything else the Britons preserved a fresh, primitive type.[2] They had not gone the way of the Gaulish Celts who had been rather blighted than blessed by a modicum of conventional civilization.[3]

In the southern part of the island, however, some advance had been made as has been shown already, upon the savage life of the Germans and old Celts. Some of the tribes not only used a gold coinage as a medium of exchange, but also showed considerable skill in agriculture. "They had learned to make a permanent separation of arable and pasture land and to apply manure appropriate to each kind of field."[4]

In the interior of the island the people set small store by the fruits of the ground. Everywhere the Romans found beneath a dark and rainy sky an endless tangle of forests and marshes, "little better than a cold and watery desert."[5] The wealth of the inhabitants consisted in their splendid herds of cattle.[6] In the growing trade with the continent after Caesar's invasion, cattle as well as the skins of the wild-beasts which swarmed in the island began to be exported in ever greater numbers. The Catuelauni profited so much by their new trade that they even submitted to Roman duties on their exports and imports, though they never paid the tribute imposed by Caesar.[7]

The Roman invasions initiated a period of healthy growth and prosperity for the southern Britons. Their capacity for civilization showed itself by the way in

1. Tac. Ann. XIV. 35; Agr. 16. 1. Cp. Mommsen, Hist. IV. 279 for the Gauls.   2. Cp. Dio LXII. 2 ff.
3. Caes. VI. 24. Cp. Froude, Caes. 216.   4. Elton, p. 119.
5. Dio LX. 19 end, LX. 20 end. Caes. V. 21. Elton, p. 223. Cp. Tac. Germ. 5 for Germany.
6. Caes. V. 21. Cp. Tac. Germ. 5 for the Germans.   7. Strabo IV. 5. 3.

which they improved their coinage and worked their iron mines hitherto undeveloped. Best of all they showed themselves capable of political organization. It was the kings of the Catuelauni who led in creating a degree of national feeling among the British tribes stronger than had ever developed in Gaul, and made possible the stout resistance that was opposed to the subsequent conquest of the island by the armies of the Roman emperors.

CHAPTER IV.

THE MISTAKE OF CLAUDIUS.

The tribute fixed by Julius Caesar to be paid annually to Rome was probably never paid.[1] For a time British chiefs ministered to the pride of Augustus the new monarch of Rome by sending embassies with presents to dedicate upon the Capitol.[2] But this practice fell off under Tiberius. Not even the Roman protectorate established by Caesar over the Trinovantes was long respected. It would appear that the Dubnovelaunus who took refuge at the court of Augustus[3] was a Trinovantian prince expelled by Tasciovanus, king of the Catuelauni.[4] Under Cunobellinus the son of Tasciovanus, the Trinovantes had been so far reconciled to the Catuelaunian supremacy that Cunobellinus made their chief town Camulodunum his capital.[5]

Officially, however, Britain was regarded as tributary to Rome.[6] Like Germany[7] and Armenia it was a potential if not actual province. It has been a common idea from the days of Tacitus to the present that Augustus was thoroughly conservative as to extension of territory and that he set what he meant to be permanent limits to the empire.[8] Nothing could be farther from the truth. Probably no single Roman added so large a territory to the empire as did Augustus. Western Germany, Raetia, Noricum, Illyria, the

---

1. Mommsen, Hist. IV. 315 and Dio LIII. 25.
2. Strabo IV. 5. 3.   3. Mon. Ancyr. VI. 2. Cp. coins.
4. Coins of Tasciovanus as late as 13 B. C. Evans, p. 223.
5. Dio LX. 21.   6. Livy, Epit. 105. Messalla, De Prog. Aug. 35. etc.
7. Mon. Ancyr. V. 11; VI. 3.
8. Tac. Ann. I. 11. 7; Agr. 13. Cp. Ranke III. 29. Schiller, Nero p. 414; Gesch. I. 214, "Grundsatz das Reich nicht durch Eroberungen zu mehren." Mommsen, Prov. I. 185, intimates that Julius Caesar had already established the Rhine as the boundary of the empire, and so Augustus only followed him. See also Momm. Hist. IV. 585.

Balkan peninsula and Egypt were won under his auspices.[1] The great mistake of his earlier policy was the attempt to extend Roman jurisdiction too rapidly, before the empire had digested and assimilated the new provinces of Gaul and Illyria.

The first aim of the new imperial policy had been to organize the offensive strength of the empire,[2] to solidify the province of Gaul and to fortify Italy at its weak point by the establishment of a scientific frontier in the north. As soon as Augustus had set up the new constitution, arranged the administration and restored the finances, the Elbe and the Danube became the immediate objective points of a grand forward movement. Germany was already well in hand, when in 6 A. D. occurred the terrible revolt of the Pannonians and Illyrians. During the next three years the new province of Germany was denuded of the tried troops and efficient commanders transferred to Illyria.[3] The Germans took advantage of a weak governor and a weak garrison, and freed themselves by annihilating at one stroke three Roman legions. True these legions were mostly raw troops and in all probability not nearly up to the normal strength.[4] But to the Roman mind a legion was a legion. The defeat of Varus caused such a tremor of grief and fear to pass through the whole Roman world, that although Germany had been reduced almost to a regular province and subjected to the tax and levy,[5] Augustus now gave it up and acknowledged the Rhine, for the present at least, as the actual frontier of the empire.

"The great object of Augustus' life was to justify

---

1. Mon. Ancyr. V. 9-VI. 49.
2. Tac. Ann. I. 9 "connexa inter se." Cp. pp. 28-29 above.
3. Schiller I. p. 229.
4. Schiller pp. 229, 232. The Roman historians with the natural preference for "losing by a mile" to losing by an inch, magnify the disaster. Cp. Livy on Cannae. 5. Schiller I. 229.

his power by showing the necessity of it. His alarm over the defeat of Varus was caused by fear for his system, which only existed because of the need for strong administrative and military centralization."[1] Augustus had cast his net too wide and the strain of simultaneous risings in Germany and Pannonia well nigh broke it. His alarm therefore for his system added to the growing feebleness of old age made him abandon the stern old Roman principle of never retreating, in spite of losses and failing finances, after a defeat. He knew that it would be many a day yet before the complete pacification of Gaul and the Danube provinces would permit the Roman eagles to be again planted on the banks of the Elbe. Accordingly his dying counsel to Tiberius was to husband the resources of the empire by confining his energies to solidifying and harmonizing the administration within the Rhine and Danube frontiers.[2] Germany remained in theory a province of the empire,[3] as the constitution of the two German skeleton provinces, and the hold which was kept on the right bank of the Rhine prove.[4] The German tribes were confronted with a standing menace. It was evident to them that when the time came, the Roman government would execute the policy of Caesar for the complete subjugation of the northern tribes, both Celts and Germans.[5]

As for an immediate conquest of Britain, nothing was farther from the intentions of Augustus and Tiberius. Though the island was in theory tributary to Rome, its actual acquisition was a far less vital need than the advance of the Rhine and Raetian frontier to the Elbe. Still, Augustus did not even on the shore of the ocean fix a limit beyond which the empire should

---

1. Seeley, Lect. Rom. Imp. I. Cp. Ranke III. 20.
2. Tac. Ann. I. 11. 7. 3. Cp. Tac. Ann. II. 26, " rebellium."
4. Tac. Ann. VI. 19. 5. Caes. B. G. VI. 9.

never go. Because he was the first to arrange a scientific frontier, with a connected system of defences, and because this frontier in its main lines actually did prove to be the permanent boundary of the empire, it has been falsely said of Augustus that he intended this frontier to be forever unchanged. Rather Augustus hoped and expected that in due time the Elbe would replace the Rhine as the actual frontier of the empire, as the Rhine had replaced the Alps and the Rhone. In the same way he never renounced the theoretical authority of Rome beyond the Strait of Dover.

But while it was officially recognized that Britain might some day be incorporated in the empire, its acquisition was distinctly not an immediate issue. Augustus amused the poets and men without political insight by his several feints at expeditions to Britain, [1] the western end of the world, and to Parthia in the extreme east.[2] The frequent mention of the British and Parthian expeditions in the same breath by the courtier poets does not imply[3] that the annexation of Britain was imminent or necessary. On the contrary it shows the shadowy character of Augustus' claims to suzerainty over the Britons.[4] Theoretically Rome ruled the whole world.[5] The statement that the imperial policy " was to fill rather than to extend,"[6] is therefore consistent with annexations of fresh territory to the domain of actual administration. Rome being practically mistress of only a portion of the world, such annexations of territory were of course a " filling," in theory, though actually an extension. This would be especially true

---

1. 34 B. C. (Dio XLIX. 38), 27 B. C. (Dio LIII. 22), and 26 B. C. (Dio LIII. 25). Dio seems doubtful of Augustus' sincerity — LIII. 22, "pretending that he was even going to invade Britain."
2. Hor Carm. I. 12, 53 ; III. 2. 3, etc.   3. As Huebner says, R. H. W. p. 10.
4. Cp. Mon. Ancyr. V. 54—VI. 2, collocation of Parthian and British refugees.
5. Cp. Momm. Prov. II, 93, Schiller I. 777, and Mon. Ancyr. V. 9—VI. 12.
6. Momm. Prov. I. 188.

of Germany, where Rome had once actually governed, and where the two skeleton provinces along both banks of the Rhine awaited "filling," just as later the province of Britain theoretically bounded by the ocean,[1] was long governed only in small part, held by the rim as it were. The scientific frontier along the Rhine and the Danube was not to be a barrier to Roman growth, but like the wall of Hadrian in Britain should permit the present development of Roman culture behind it, and its future expansion beyond it. But the idea of an actual subjugation of Britain was with Augustus and Tiberius no more and no less hazy than the purpose of extending Roman administration over Parthia or India. If envoys came from Britain to offer homage to the master of the world, they came also from India.[2] Much more immediate was the necessity of ensuring the isolation of Gaul and the safety of Italy by the subjugation of Germany.

As a matter of fact, Strabo a man of keen, logical insight, presents clearly the practical attitude of Augustus towards Britain.[3] He says that the Romans having ascertained the poverty of Britain and its worthlessness whether for economic purposes or for the strategic requirements of the empire, seeing that the Britons could do no harm to Gaul, and that the cost of an occupation of the island would so far balance the tribute to be derived from so poor a people, that the actual gain if any would not be equal to the existing tariff revenue from British trade, voluntarily relinquished the ephemeral conquests of Caesar and the dangers of maintaining them.[4]

Tiberius quite agreed with the views of Augustus.[5]

1. See Tac. Ann. XIV. 29. 1 "subiecturum ei *provinciam* fuisse."
2. Mon. Ancyr. V. 50.   3. II. 5. 8; IV. 5. 3.
4. Cp. Appian (Proem. 5) who wrote a hundred years after the Claudian invasion.
5. Tac. Agr. 13. Huebner's interpretation of "consilium id divus Augustus vocabat" (Hermes, XVI, p 517) is wrong. Cp. Tac. Ann. I. 11 end, and Mommsen, Prov. I. 187 n. 1. See also Gibbon, Vol. I. ch. I.

With his contempt for popular applause, he did not even pretend to be thinking about conquests in Britain or the far east. He continued Augustus' later policy of carefully consolidating the new empire, leaving to a successor the task of realizing the aim of Augustus' foreign policy, the shortening of the frontier line, bulwarking of Italy, and removal of the great masses of the army farther from Rome. While this great end awaited consummation, it is inconceivable that Tiberius "recognized the obligation of conquering in Britain."[1]

Meanwhile trade had become so flourishing between Britain and the mainland that the revenue from customs in this quarter must have been quite considerable. Even the besotted Caligula could not bring himself to make such a leap into the dark as to exile a large portion of his best troops to a distant island,[2] merely to gratify his own vanity and the city rabble's craving for sensation. His finances were in a ruinous condition as it was.[3] By listening to the petition of Adminius, the banished son of King Cunobellinus who took refuge with him in Gaul,[4] and undertaking a costly and perilous expedition to Britain, he had sufficient sense to see that his treasury might be completely wrecked. Besides Caligula had still some regard left for the maxims of imperial policy laid down by Julius and Augustus.[5]

But it was reserved for Claudius, the most foolish of Roman emperors,[6] to perpetrate one of the greatest errors of imperial policy. As soon as his economy and the systematic administration of his ministers had repaired the ravages made by Caligula upon the treasury, the new emperor looked about with the mild frenzy for action which sometimes attacks the bookish man, for a

[1]. Schiller I. 319.   [2]. Cp. Mommsen, Prov. I. 188.
[3]. See Schiller I. 309 f.   [4]. Sueton. Calig. 44.
[5]. See Tac. Agr. 13 "ingentes adversus Germaniam conatus."
[6]. Cp. Huebner R. H. W. p. 10; Gibbon, Vol. I. ch. 1.

THE MISTAKE OF CLAUDIUS.

field in which he could win a military reputation.[1] Brought up rather as a scullion than as an heir of the imperial house,[2] Claudius had not been imbued with the precepts laid down by Julius and Augustus for the solidification of the empire and the advancement of its frontiers on strategic principles.[3] Gaul and the Danube Provinces were now sufficiently Romanized to allow of the long projected conquest of Germany to the Elbe.[4] Instead of bending all his energies to this work, Claudius proceeded to hit out at random in all directions.[5] But it was Britain that outbid the attractions of all other fields for the aimless enterprise of a weak-minded monarch.

Claudius and the more unreasoning portion of his subjects had perhaps not yet satisfied themselves that riches were not to be found in Britain.[6] Perhaps the increased trade may have led people to exaggerate the mineral and other wealth of the island. Even as early as thirty years after Caesar's unprofitable expeditions, Strabo had thought it necessary to correct popular misapprehensions about Britain. Probably the ideas of the masses in 43 A. D. stood in more desperate need of confutation. At any rate Claudius undertook in that year his great invasion of Britain, chiefly in order to get popularity by meeting an old demand of the rabble, which had been fostered by poets and dreamers ever since the days of Julius Caesar. He knew that with the time and armies at his disposal he could accomplish more in the island than was possible for Caesar in his

---

1. Sueton. Claud. 17.   2. Sueton. Claud. 2 6.
3. Cp. Ranke III. 100 "eigentlich gegen die Grundsatze des Augustus und des Tiberius."
4. Cp. Furneaux, Tac. Ann. II. p. 130.   5. Orosius VII. 6. 9.
6. Cp. Huebner, R. H. W. p. 10 "diess Ruhm und Schaetze versprechende Unternehmen." Cp. Cox in Arch. Journ. LII. p. 26. Mela and Tacitus both felt called upon to justify the conquest from an economic standpoint. Mela (III. 50) politely expresses his doubts by intimating that Britain's products are suitable rather for cattle than for men. Tac. Agr. 12 "pretium victoriae."

two short campaigns. The senate and people would therefore magnify his exploits, setting him higher than the great Julius himself.[1]

Germany, on the other hand, was a land of ill omen to the popular mind,[2] and probably Claudius' own superstition made him shrink from invading the land which had engulfed so many Roman legions. Besides, one of the reasons that had made the conquest of Germany seem necessary to Augustus was no longer cogent. Since the avenging campaigns of Germanicus the Germans had shown great respect for the Rhine boundary of Gaul. The Gauls undisturbed by German inroads or intrigues had resigned themselves to the government of Rome, and were rapidly becoming assimilated to their conquerors. It was only after 60,000 picked troops had been transferred to Britain that the Germans again ventured to attack the empire.[3] But when Corbulo had beaten them back and established Roman authority far into the heart of their country, Claudius renounced Germany for good and withdrew the legions across the Rhine from even the narrow strip on the right bank which had been held since the time of Drusus.[4] Perhaps he could not do otherwise after wasting the men and money of the empire in conquering an "alter orbis."[5] But it is doubtful whether Claudius gave a thought to the real import of this retreat from the policy of Augustus for the future of Rome. In the small vanity of his British victory he was incapable of understanding how he was drawing out the long thin line of his frontier forces, when he should have taken steps to shorten and thicken

---

1. Claudius doubtless encouraged a contemptuous view of Caesar's campaigns. See Lucan II. 572; Anthol. Lat. (Riese) No. 423. Mela III. 49. Orosius VII. 6. 9. Cp. Revue Archeologique II. Ser. XXXI. p. 104.
2. Cp. the story in Dio LV. 1.   3. Tac. Ann. XI. 18.
4. Schiller I. 323. Huebner R. H. W. p. 113.
5. In spite of his increase of the number of the legions from 25 to 27. See Jung, p. 276.

THE MISTAKE OF CLAUDIUS. 57

it. Still less did he see that he was leaving Raetia, the slight bulwark of Italy, open to barbarians who would one day burst through and quench the light of Roman civilization. The theory of Rome's universal hegemony was now of the past. The deeds of Drusus and Tiberius which had wafted the terror of Rome's name to the far off tribes by the Baltic Sea were forgotten for the paltry and precarious foothold which one of the finest armies Rome ever sent forth gained among the uncouth, brave inhabitants of Britain.[1]

It can not be said[2] that the conquest of Britain promised to be easier than that of Germany. Julius Caesar had been impressed with the courage and warlike character of the British tribes.[3] Like the Britons, the Germans were tall and huge, but in spite of their bodily strength no match for disciplined Roman armies.[4] The victory of Marius was as decisive as any won by Agricola. In three years (12-9 B. C.) Drusus conquered more territory in Germany than Roman generals won in Britain during thirty years after the invasion of Claudius. The annexation of western Germany would have been still easier in 43 A. D.[5] Britain was as difficult to traverse, by reason of forests and marshes as Germany.[6] The Celtic tribes both continental and insular were perhaps harder to assimilate when conquered than the Germans. But Claudius was bent not on so common-place and hackneyed an enterprise as the conquest of Germany. The subjugation of Britain, while quite as difficult and hazardous as that of Germany, promised exaltation for its promoter at the expense of his predecessor Julius Caesar, and possibly prizes for the speculators and usurers.

1. Mela III. 49.   2. With Schiller I. 352.
3. Cp. Jung p. 274, and see Herodian III. 7. 6.
4. Cp. Tac. Ann. II. 14.
5. As evidenced by Corbulo's success there. Schiller I. 323.
6. See above p. 47, n. 5.

But this advance of Roman power across the English Channel has been generally admired as the masterly execution of a move which had always been held to be inevitable by Roman statesmen since the time of Julius Caesar.[1] Some say that the Gauls could never have been reconciled to Roman government while their kinsmen, the insular Celts, having in their midst the centre of the religion of the entire Celtic race, remained free.[2] Others are tormented with imaginings of not only a bad British influence among the Gallic Celts, but armed descents upon the north coast.[3] No one is ready with an inventory of the positive economic or military or political advantages which the occupation of Britain seemed to hold out to Claudius. It was then a necessity, and a hard necessity, the better horn of a dilemma, snatched at only to save northern Gaul for Rome. One writer, instinctively aware of the difficulty of his position, fancies that Tacitus saw in this action of a half Celt anxious to complete the subjugation of the Celtic race a miracle which could only be explained as the intervention of fate to bring Vespasian to the front as commander of a legion in the expedition.[4]

If only there had been a Celtic nation bound together like the Grecian states by a common blood, language and religion, these reasonings might almost persuade. And while it is now generally accepted that the inhabitants of the British Isles were of the same race as those of Gaul, the ancients did not suspect this fact. Tacitus hesitatingly suggests that the Belgic Britons of the extreme south-east, "nearest to Gaul," were of Gaulish stock.[5] The origin of the tribes north

---

[1.] See Mommsen, Prov. I. 188.   Schiller I. 319.   Huebner R. H. W. p. 10.
[2.] See above, p. 8, n. 2.   Add Spooner, Tac. Hist. p. 38.
[3.] Huebner R. H. W. p. 12.
[4.] Huebner R. H. W. p. 11.
[5.] Tac. Agr. 11. He follows Caes. V. 12.

of these he declared to be uncertain.¹ No Roman emperor therefore could have dreamed of annexing Britain on ethnological grounds. Or why was Hibernia not annexed? To say nothing of the Semites of Mesopotamia, the Dacians of Russia, the Egyptians of the Upper Nile, or shall we add the Aryans of India and the Turanians of China and North America? Our philologists have failed to advocate the conquest of the trans-Rhenane Germans, though here they have a good case, as the Romans knew well the relationship of the German tribes on both sides of the Rhine. But this idea of the rounding off of the conquest of the Celtic race seems to be not far from absurd.

The question of a national Druidic religion has already been disposed of. A common religion must seem an impossibility almost without any special proof. The isolation of Britain is and always was a geographical and historical fact.² The soldiers of Aulus Plautius mutinied when ordered to Britain not because they were going against brother Celts, but because they were to be banished as it were off the earth.³ Those who assume the existence two thousand years ago of a national feeling, a national religion and an active commercial intercourse holding Britain and Gaul so closely together as to render the conquest of the continental Celts insecure without the subjugation of Britain strive against the verdict of all history and against the judgment of nature herself.

To assert that Gaul could never have been Romanized without the occupation of Britain is to fly in the face of the facts. Gaul had already been deeply permeated with Roman civilization. During the

---
1. Tac. Agr. 11. Cp. Germ. 45, where Tac. speaks of a German tribe speaking a language like the British. This is perhaps erroneous, but it shows that Tac. distinguished sharply between the bulk of the British population and the Gauls.
2. Cp. Freeman's whole essay "Alter Orbis."   3. Dio LX. 19.

twenty-two years since the revolt of 21 A. D., which occurring among inland tribes could not have been encouraged by British sympathy, the country had in all quietness grown reconciled to its new condition. Its complete assimilation was now only a question of time.[1] That the conquest of Britain was achieved chiefly by Gallic troops is proof enough how little sympathy existed between the insular and the continental Celts.

If the north coast of Gaul was liable to attack from Britain, Strabo must have been greatly mistaken when he wrote that "the Britons could do no injury to us."[2] The Britons were by no means seafaring people. No ancient writer records a tendency shown by the Britons to meddle in any way with the Romans on the mainland. On the other hand they had on one occasion rescued and restored to their country Roman soldiers cast on the British shore by a storm.[3] This friendly act betokens no longing on the part of the islanders to trouble the coast of Gaul with buccaneering expeditions. And even if danger had threatened Gaul from Britain and not from Germany, as was actually the case, it had been far less expensive to make simply a punitive expedition to the island occasionally, at least until the continental policy of Caesar and Augustus had been carried out.

All the usual arguments therefore for the advisedness of Claudius' expedition of conquest rest on the flimsiest sort of foundations. Britain the "Alter Orbis" lay apart from the continental system of Rome. It was only the old blind impulse to conquest for conquest's sake[4] which actuated Claudius, and on which as the leading motive of the urban rabble he could count for the praise of his successes.

---

[1] Cp. Jung p. 200. See Strabo IV. 1. 2, and IV. 4. 2, cited by Arnold, Later Roman Commonwealth, p. 491. [2] II. 5. 8.
[3] Tac. Ann. II. 24 (16 A. D.)   [4] Cp. Ranke III. 5.

THE MISTAKE OF CLAUDIUS.

Perhaps the most convincing bit of evidence against the racial and religious hypothesis, next to the fact that no ancient writer made bold to attribute to Claudius' expedition any other motive than that of self-aggrandizement, is furnished by a passage of Dio Cassius. In Book LIII. 22 he gives as the reason why Augustus did not invade Britain in 27 B. C. the unsettled state of Gaul.[1] If British influence or sympathy had contributed to hinder the pacification of Gaul, as German influence certainly did,[2] Augustus would have been stimulated to invade Britain, not deterred. Evidently Augustus and also Dio Cassius believed that Germany, not Britain, must be conquered in the best interests of Gaul and the whole empire. The very reason assigned by modern writers for the necessity of attacking Britain is preferred by Dio as the reason why Augustus did not attack the island.

Claudius therefore in abandoning all the traditions of previous imperial policy consulted nothing else than his own vanity. He seized the first opportunity that appeared for a great military expedition. Bericus,[3] an exiled British chief, perhaps overcome by the power of Caratacus or Togodumnus, the sons of Cunobellinus recently dead, came to Claudius and had no difficulty in persuading him to send a force into Britain.[4] It seems also that the two sons of Cunobellinus, the aged monarch who had held sway over southern Britain for nearly thirty years,[5] foolishly provoked the Romans by "demanding in not very diplomatic form the extradition of Bericus."[6]

---

1. No ancient writer says that Britain was conquered in order to secure Gaul.
2. See Schiller I. 214.
3. Mommsen and Huebner are wrong in identifying Bericus with Verica, the British chief of Silchester. Verica's coinage is of much earlier date. See Rhys, C. B. p. 23.   4. Dio LX. 19.   5. Rhys, pp. 26, 35.
6. Jung, p. 275.

Claudius quickly collected a powerful army under the command of Aulus Plautius[1] and made ready to send the flower of his troops into a land which in later days, though civilized and improved by a long Roman occupation, the Goths disdained to conquer and Charlemagne was content to leave to itself.[2]

1. Dio IX. 19, etc.
2. See Freeman's essay " Alter Orbis."

CHAPTER V.

THE CLAUDIAN INVASION.

Aulus Plautius, the commander chosen for the expedition, was probably at the time of his appointment (43 A. D.) in charge of Gallia Belgica, or possibly of one of the German provinces on the Rhine.[1] He seems to have been one of the best generals available for a difficult undertaking. The selection of the officers for the campaign was in the hands of Narcissus the freedman minister of Claudius,[2] and it was his excellent judgment assisted doubtless by Plautius' special knowledge in arranging all the details of the expedition that made it so speedily successful.

The armament was a very elaborate one. Four splendid legions, the Second Augusta, Twentieth Valeria Victrix, and Fourteenth Gemina from the Rhine, and the Ninth Hispana from Pannonia, commanded by such legates as Vespasian (of the Second Augusta) and Hosidius Geta, were gathered together, with perhaps a detachment of the Eighth Augusta also stationed on the Rhine, and about thirty thousand auxiliaries.[3] The whole array, according to Huebner, numbered upwards of 70,000 men.

When all was ready for the departure, the troops mutinied, refusing to be exiled " out of the world," for no one's profit, but to satisfy the whimsical vanity of a foolish emperor.[4] Though the ignorant mob of the City may have expected in some vague way a share in

---

1. See Furneaux p. 132 note 4.   2. Dio LX. 19. Sueton. Vesp. 4.
3. Dio LX. 20. Tac. Hist. III. 44. Josephus B. J. II. 16. etc. See Huebner, Exercitus Britannicus, in Hermes XVI. cp C. I. L. VII. pp. 5, 305. The inscriptions quoted do not prove that the Eighth Augusta or part of it went to Britain.   4. Dio LX. 19.

the fruits of victory over possibly rich nations, and certainly looked forward to the largesses which a successful emperor would be sure to distribute, the army which may be supposed to have preserved traditions of the fruitless hardships undergone by Julius Caesar's men, did not deceive itself as to what lay before it.[1] In Gaul, too, the home of most of the legionaries, since the new commerce with Britain had made the island better known, people were well aware that no portable booty was to be got by the soldier.

Plautius being unable to put down the mutiny himself, Narcissus came to the army and discipline was soon restored. The whole force set sail after the long delay caused by the mutiny, probably from Gesoriacum (Boulogne), Caesar's Portus Itius. At first the wind was unfavorable, but finally the army landed, following the course of Julius Caesar, in all probability near the present Romney Marsh.[2] Perhaps the Britons had heard of the mutiny and did not expect the landing, for it took place unopposed.[3] But they were not long idle, after the news of the invasion had spread. Caratacus and Togodumnus held the numerous cantons of southern Britain well together and made the Romans earn every inch of their advance.

Some have thought that the Roman march was directed northward from a place afterwards named Clausentum, situated close to modern Southampton, or from Venta (Winchester) "the first seat of the Roman command."[4] The arguments for this view are: (1) The excellence of the harbor of Southampton (Ptolemy's "Great Harbor") must have been early perceived by the Romans. (2) The Roman road running from

---

1. Cp. Merivale VI. 18.
2. Huebner, R. H. W. p. 17. It is not necessary to suppose with Guest (Orig. Celt. II. 399 *ff.*) that the three divisions of the force mentioned by Dio landed far apart from one another.   3. Dio LX. 19.
4. Huebner R. H. W. p. 19; Hermes XVI. pp. 528-529.

Clausentum through Venta (Winchester) and Calleva (Silchester) to Londinium was probably first laid by the engineers of Plautius with a view to the systematic conquest of the country, from the base in Cogidubnus' kingdom at the centre of the south coast. (3) King Cogidubnus of the Regni, a tribe about the modern Chichester, was the faithful friend and ally of the Romans from the first time of the invasion of Plautius down to the reign of Vespasian.[1] His services were rewarded with a bestowal of territory and the title of "Legatus Augusti" added to that of "Rex." The state of the Regni, then, was used by the Romans, following their fixed custom, as a fulcrum and as a decoy, like the "friendly tribes" of North American Indians two centuries ago. At Chichester the old seat of Cogidubnus, several epigraphical monuments remain from the earliest time of the Roman occupation, showing the importance of the early relations with the Regni for the Roman cause.[2] It has therefore been supposed that the Romans first established themselves at Venta near Chichester, founding Clausentum as a naval station on one of the best natural harbors in the world.[3]

According to Huebner the leading exponent of this theory, the Isle of Wight commanding the entrance to the harbor of Southampton was one of the first conquests made by the Romans.[4] He then traces their march along the above mentioned road to Venta and thence to Calleva. Here we are to suppose that Plautius already acquainted with the configuration of the western and eastern coasts of England, deeply indented by the estuaries of the Severn and the Thames, resolved to proceed as it were by degrees of

1. Tac. Agr. 14. C. I. L. VII. 11.   2. See esp. C. I. L. VII. 11.
3. The Venta inscription (C. I. L. VII. 5) is also used as an argument, but surely not seriously.
4. Huebner R. H. W. p. 21; Hermes XVI. 528.

latitude, conquering the land symmetrically and contemporaneously west and east.[1] While the fleet goes around Land's End to make a diversion in the mouth of the Severn, giving no heed, it may be observed, to the siren tin-mines of Cornwall, or if we are to believe Diodorus (or Posidonius?) and his modern disciples,[2] to its gentle, conquest-inviting inhabitants, Plautius struck into the territory of the Dobuni, fought and won a great battle at the Avon River, and almost immediately afterwards appeared at the heels of the Britons near the mouth of the Thames, supported at this point also by a division of the fleet.[3] Here he halts, surely out of breath, waiting for Claudius to join the army. Claudius arrived, the troops impetuously clear the river and press forward to Camulodunum, the seat of the dominant dynasty of the Catuelauni.

The objections to this view, however, are overwhelming. To the first argument for the harbor of Southampton as the early station of the Roman fleet, supporting a base of operations near Clausentum, the answer is that the Romans probably landed near Romney, and certainly always preferred a nearer port to a more remote though better one.[4] It was at Portus Lemanae, near Romney, that the "Classis Britannica" afterwards had its head-quarters,[5] not at Clausentum. As for the Roman road running from Clausentum to Londinium, it is only necessary to recall that a road also ran from Lemanae to Londinium through Durovernum (Canterbury). If Plautius' engineers built their roads intelligently, we can hardly imagine that they started from any other point than Lemanae, the landing place and per-

---

[1]. Huebner R. H. W. p 20; also "Gloucester the Roman Glevum," a paper in the Transactions of the Cotteswold Club.
[2]. E. g. Edwards, p. 85 in Traill's Social England.
[3]. Huebner R. H. W. pp. 20-21.
[4]. Cp. Furneaux p. 135 n. 3. The three great entrances to Britain in Roman times were Rutupiae, Dubris and Lemanae. See C. R. Smith, Arch. Cantiana XVIII, p. 41. [5]. C. I. L. VII. 18, 1226.

manent head-quarters of the fleet. The third argument of the Chichester base is of no weight, for Cogidubnus could surely have assisted the Romans in Kent as well as in Hampshire.

But the immediate building of a road from Clausentum to Calleva, followed by an excursion into the territories of the Dobuni (about Gloucester) would seem to convict Plautius of a laughable uncertainty of purpose. The unifying power in the British resistance was the unquestioned supremacy of the Catuelaunian princes Togodumnus and Caratacus.[1] The capital of their realm was Camulodunum.[2] This then should and must have been the object of Plautius' attack. That he should have wandered off to the Severn River to worry some petty dependency of the Catuelauni instead of straightway aiming at the very heart of the British resistance appears impossible. And further the assumption that the Romans set out to conquer the island by a symmetrical advance northward in the west and the east is wholly unwarranted. It is fairly certain that the conquest proceeded from the beginning far more speedily in the east than in the west.[3] Nothing could have been more natural. The eastern part of Britain must have been much more densely populated, and the difficulties of conquest were nothing to those presented by the mountainous west. The centre of power was at Camulodunum in Essex,[4] afterwards the capital of the "provincia," and the Romans as we know[5] lost no time in closing with Togodumnus and Caratacus, the result of their overthrow being as Plautius expected the annihilation of the united British resistance.

Perhaps the most untenable part of Huebner's theory is his conjecture that the Roman fleet sailed

---
[1]. Cp. Edwards in "Social England" I. 7-8.   [2]. Dio LX. 20.
[3]. Mommsen Prov. I. 193. Ruggiero, Diz. Epigr. I. p. 1030b.
[4]. See Tac. Ann. XII. 37.   [5]. Dio LX. 20.

along the east and west coasts to aid the operations of the land army. It is impossible to believe that the Romans knew the way around Land's End to the mouth of the Severn at this time. There is every reason to believe that they entirely neglected the south-western corner of the island then and for long afterwards.[1] The fleet *may* have sailed along the east coast to the Thames, but there is not the slightest ground for saying that it did.[2]

The only reasonable view of the course taken by Plautius is that adopted by Merivale and Mommsen. The landing of the Romans at Lemanae was followed by a march not to the Isle of Wight, the Severn and other outlying places, but straight upon Camulodunum through Kent and Surrey.

It is probable that Cogidubnus became almost immediately attached to the Roman cause. One of the first acts of Plautius, according to Dio, was to secure the alliance of the Boduni, a tribe whose prince was the vassal of the Catuelaunian kings. An ingenious and plausible suggestion has been made that these Boduni, wrongly identified by Huebner and others with the Dobuni, but placed by Mommsen in the south-east part of England, were the tribe ruled over by Cogidubnus and known later to the Romans as the Regni.[3] The invasion must have at once tempted Cogidubnus, doubtless a disaffected vassal, to join issues with the foreign foe against the native domination of the Catuelauni. Dio also says that a garrison was left among the

---

1. Momm. Prov. I. 193. Huebner R. H. W. 17.

2. Cp. notes 1 and 2 to pp. 69 and 72 below. The naval triumph of Claudius must be referred simply to the boast of conquering the ocean, and not to important co-operation of the fleet with the land force.

3. Furneaux p. 135 n. 1. Cp. Rhys C.B. p. 300—" Regni—probably more correctly Regnii, a derivative from regnum. That is the state of Cogidubnus who as the ally of the Romans was permitted to retain his title of king, was *par excellence* the regnum and its people the Regnii, their Celtic name being forgotten."

Boduni, which while probable enough of the tribe under Cogidubnus, would be impossible for the Dobuni of Gloucestershire who were independent some time afterwards. But Cogidubnus, whether king of the Boduni or not, very early threw in his lot with the Romans and possibly gave good assistance to Plautius in his march to the Thames.

After the submission of the Boduni, the Romans advanced to a certain river, perhaps the Medway, and forced the passage in a lively fight in which Vespasian distinguished himself.[1] The next day the Britons rallied and opposed a stubborn resistance to the Roman advance. But in spite of the most unyielding valor that had confronted the Romans since the Punic wars, they were defeated with heavy loss, chiefly owing to a brilliant and daring manoeuvre of Hosidius Geta.[2]

The patriot army now somewhat discouraged retreated sullenly and slowly to the Thames, crossing it near the mouth.[3] Plautius pressed forward as rapidly as he dared, and attempted to pass the river. But the Britons at first succeeded in repulsing him. On a second trial the Romans overcame all obstacles, rushing the British position on the north bank and driving the natives into the marshes.[4] Many were killed on both sides. Togodumnus died fighting, but his spirit still lived in his brother Caratacus. The fury of the Britons at the loss of their prince nerved them for a moment to so determined a resistance that Plautius thought best to halt his troops and strengthen his hold on the territory already won. He sent for the emperor, as Claudius had ordered him to do in case any serious emergency should arise.[5] Probably after all Plautius merely

---
1. Dio LX. 20. Cp. Merivale VI. 22. 2. Dio LX. 20.
3. Probably at London. See Furneaux p. 136 n. 2.
4. Dio LX. 20. Not a word is said of any help rendered by the fleet at this juncture. 5. Dio LX. 21.

wished to gratify the emperor by giving him a chance
to pretend that by taking the field himself he had
snatched victory from defeat.[1] Plautius knew that his
game was won. Encamped on the north bank of the
Thames,[2] he was within striking distance of Camulo
dunum. Nothing remained but to traverse a level
tract of a few miles.

The progress of the Roman army, considering the
fierceness of the British fighting, had been quite rapid.
Claudius left Rome about July or August 43 A. D.
and Plautius must have crossed the Thames and sent
the message some weeks before that.[3] While the
emperor was on his way to Britain, Plautius probably
pushed on the work of building roads, improving his
connections and tightening his grip on the conquered
territory.

Journeying with all haste, Claudius reached Britain
early in autumn accompanied by several distinguished
officers, Galba, Valerius Asiaticus, L. Junius Silanus,
Cn. Pompeius Magnus, Cn. Sentius Saturninus and
others.[4] It is not certain that Claudius did not bring
with him the detachment of the Eighth Augusta from
Mayence, or other reinforcements.[5] Perhaps some of
the auxiliaries enumerated by Huebner first came to
Britain with Claudius.[6] But the evidence for the military details of this whole campaign is so scanty that it
is not possible to say with certainty that the Eighth
Augusta or part of it went to Britain at all.

If Claudius did bring more troops with him, they
were not needed. While Plautius was waiting for the

---

1. See Merivale VI. 22.
2. That Claudius crossed the Thames without trouble means that Plautius
held the north bank.
3. Dio LX. 23. Cp. Furneaux p. 136. Plautius could hardly have conquered the Isle of Wight and a large part of western England so soon, as
Huebner thinks.   4. See Huebner's list, Hermes XVI.
5. Cp. above p. 63 n. 3.   6. Cp. Schiller I. 320.

emperor's arrival, the Britons had time to reflect a little on their defeats and the inevitable power of their enemy. The first sting of passionate grief at the death of Togodumnus once abated, the courage of the natives must have been relaxed, and hearts that once trusted for victory to the fallen hero would recoil in dismay from another conflict with his conqueror. Probably some princes now went over to the Romans, making the best terms they could for themselves. Even Caratacus, feeling himself helpless to avert the fate of his people and moved to despair at the loss of his brother, seems to have retired to his dependencies in the west, abandoning all attempt to check the progress of the legions to his capital.[1]

On arriving in Britain Claudius took the field in person, crossed the Thames and advanced upon Camuodunum without meeting any serious opposition.[2] The town fell immediately and with it the organizing force of the Catuelaunian hegemony. Caratacus still remained a powerful opponent of the Romans in the west, but he was now a prince without a city, influential only through the magnetism of his own personality. Henceforth the several British tribes fought singlehanded with the Romans or with each other, and one at a time were subdued or submitted to the foreign yoke.[3]

Claudius stayed in the island just long enough to constitute Britain a province of the empire and install Plautius as first governor. The annexation of Britain was perhaps not formally ratified by the senate until the following year, 44.[4] Claudius returned to the continent after spending only sixteen days in Britain, and of this time not more than a week or ten days at most north of the Thames.[5]

1. Tac. Ann. XII. 33. 2. Sueton. Claud. 17. C. I. L. VI. 920.
3. Tac. Agr. 12, 32. 4. Dio LX. 23. 5. Dio LX. 23.

The emperor was hugely pleased at the outcome of his expedition. As soon as he returned to Rome, in the early part of 44 A. D., he celebrated a grand triumph and showered distinctions and promotions upon those who had helped him to success. The cringing senate shouted praises for its happy ruler till it must have almost come to really believe in him. His infant son received the name Britannicus. In order to facilitate the conquest of Britain, the measures which Claudius or his lieutenant Aulus Plautius might take were allowed to be valid without the sanction of the senate. An arch of triumph was erected over the Via Flaminia in Rome.[1] Poets proclaimed the conquest of the ocean,[2] and Claudius himself toyed with this conceit, celebrating a naval triumph in the Adriatic.[3] In the emotional hurrahs that rang throughout the empire,[4] there was no place for the logical considerations of policy. The citizens were glad to know that the aggressive power of Rome was still vigorous. As reports of the wealth of Britain in lead and iron mines came to the business centres, the joy of conquest became more pointed. Nobody cared anything about a blunder of statesmanship, for nobody then believed that a thousand mistakes in policy could shake the structure of the empire.

The fatal step had been taken. Seventy thousand of Rome's best soldiers were set to the task of building roads, redeeming marshes and fighting the bravest of barbarians in a land altogether outside of the imperial frontier system. To withdraw would henceforth be next to impossible. "In military undertakings there lies an inner fatality which, once they are begun, leaves

---

[1]. Dio LX. 21-23.
[2]. Anthol. Lat. (Riese) 419-426. Cp. Hegesippus B. J. II. 9.
[3]. Pliny H. N. III 20.
[4]. Cp. Huebner R. H. W. p. 24, and Revue Archeologique II. Ser. XXXI. p. 103.

no longer any room for the consideration whether they are to be pursued further or not."[1] The Romans were now committed to the occupation of a new and distant province which their conservative spirit and indomitable tenacity would maintain for three hundred and fifty years. As an immediate result of the new conquest, the plan of Julius Caesar and Augustus for the annexation of Germany was definitely given up by Claudius,[2] and though for a moment revived by Trajan never afterwards figured prominently in the Roman foreign policy.

1. Ranke III. 198.
2. Tac. Ann. XI. 19.

CHAPTER VI.

THE BUILDING OF THE PROVINCE.

Britain was now formally enrolled among the consular provinces directly controlled by the emperor. Aulus Plautius, "Legatus Augusti pro Praetore," was assisted in the administration by the ordinary official staff. A procurator, either a knight or a freedman of the emperor,[1] represented the interests of the fiscus, a finance lord responsible directly to the emperor and though politically subordinate to the legate, to a certain degree independent in his own sphere.[2]

As in the other provinces a tribute was fixed for the subjected tribes to pay annually. The procurator drew up the usual assessment lists and probably from the very first collected the taxes immediately through his servants, often public slaves or freedmen,[3] abandoning the old mode still partially retained in other provinces, of farming out the revenues of the fiscus to publicans. No doubt those tribes which submitted to Roman rule without striking a blow for their liberty were treated with somewhat less rigor and oppression by the Roman finance officials, although "civitates liberae" and "foederatae" were subject to taxation as much as the ordinary provincials.[4] But the Catuelauni, Trinovantes and other tribes that fought for their freedom were made to feel not only the galling pressure of a regular system of taxation, always detested by an

---

1. Decianus Catus and Julius Classicianus seem to have been knights or there is no meaning in the ridicule heaped on Polyclitus (Tac. Ann. XIV. 39).
2. Cp. Tac. Agr. 15 aeque discordiam—aeque concordiam. Also Ann. XIV. 38.
3. Agr. 15 alterius servos ; 19 libertos servosque publicae rei.
4. See Unger in Leipziger Studien X. De Cens. Prov. p. 62.

uncivilized people, but also the abuses of that system, all the cruelty and extortion of which the corrupt Roman civil service was capable.

It was not the procurator and his satellites however who gave the Britons their first taste of slavery. The bravery and splendid physique of the native youth adapted them for the Roman auxiliary service. While the procurators could make little for some time out of a barbarous, uncultivated land, Plautius and his successors enforced the military conscription, drafting contingents of British auxiliaries for service in Britain and in different parts of the empire.[1]

Wherever the governor's troops went, violence and outrage were sure to follow, until the forms of the new government should have time to impress themselves upon a thoroughly pacified country. Territorially the province, or that part of the country directly administered by the governor, exclusive of the dependent principalities, was for a time somewhat vaguely defined, and certainly not very extensive. But the levy still more than the tribute applied alike to all parts of the country overawed by the legions.

Most severe for the subject people must have been the various requisitions squeezed out of them by the subactores or other officers of the governor. The Britons had to furnish a fixed annual amount of corn or other provisions for the public magazines of the province, find horses, beasts of burden, wood, fodder, etc., for the armies, and submit to the quartering of soldiers upon them.[2] All these burdens falling suddenly upon them along with the loss of their independence, and before they could begin to appreciate the law and order of Roman rule, must have filled the majority of

---
1. Tac. Agr. 18 : 31 : 32.
2. Tac. Agr. 19. Cp. Daremberg and Saglio, art. Annona.

the natives with the deepest hatred of their alien masters and tended to render very uncertain the permanence of the province.

Plautius was obliged to rule with a strong hand. Though many native princes had made their submission, among them Cogidubnus of Chichester and Prasutagus of the Iceni (in Norfolk and Suffolk), and the whole east as far north as modern Lincolnshire was therefore nominally subject to Plautius,[1] it was evident that the establishment of Roman power in the shape of a regular, just and systematic administration would not be immediately realized. The work of Plautius was to introduce Roman law and justice so far as feasible, to open up the country for imperial exploitation and private enterprise, and to make the actual limits of his jurisdiction coincide as nearly as possible with the theoretical bounds of "Britannia," that is to conquer as much of the island as he could.[2]

During the four years of his command Plautius assisted by his able lieutenant Vespasian succeeded in materially extending his dominion in the south-west. Vespasian commanding the second legion conquered the Isle of Wight and reduced two powerful tribes to submission.[3] Perhaps the Isle of Wight was part of the gift of territory with which the Romans rewarded the good services of King Cogidubnus, though it is possible that only his own rightful dominions were "presented" to him by his powerful and not too generous friends, much as the North American Indians have been "granted" reserves.[4]

---

[1]. Tac. Ann. XII. 31; XIV. 31.
[2]. Theoretically the whole island was annexed in 43 A. D. Cp. Ann. XIV. 29 subiecturum ei provinciam. The Romans annexed first and subdued afterwards—Haverfield in Arch. Journ. Vol. XLIX, p. 223.
[3]. Sueton. Vesp. 4. Dio LX. 30—The story of Titus rescuing his father is pure fiction. See Furneaux, and Sueton. Tiberius 2.
[4]. Cp. Furneaux p. 136.

It would appear that Vespasian even extended his conquests over Devonshire which was perhaps but thinly populated and therefore, as its Dumnonian inhabitants proved submissive, drew little notice from the Romans.[1] "Legend and coins alike connect the names of Isca (Exeter) and Vespasian, and the slight notices that history gives of his British exploits may lead us to believe that it was he who, while Claudius reigned, made Isca an outpost of Rome."[2]

The course of conquest under Plautius would seem to have partly followed the line which Huebner claimed for the first operations of the Claudian expedition. Between 44 and 47 A. D. the Roman columns advanced perhaps along the road from Chichester to Calleva (Silchester) and from Londinium to Calleva. Two causes would determine this line of advance. The city of Cogidubnus and Londinium must have been excellent bases for operations in the west, while the military road connecting Camulodunum, Londinium and Chichester effectively secured the south-eastern corner of the island. The second reason, which was the cause for fighting in the west rather than farther north, was that Caratacus had taken up the cudgels again and was most active in organizing a coalition of his former dependencies in the west in order to lead once more an attack upon the Romans. It is possible also that the Romans may have got news of the Somerset mines which they soon began to work.

At any rate when the extant part of Tacitus' narrative takes up the history of the British wars at the appointment of Plautius' successor P. Ostorius Scapula, we find the Romans, after many a hard won fight that

---

1. See Merivale VI. 26, n. 1 —coins of Claudius found at Exeter. Perhaps the tile of the II Augusta found at Honey Ditches (Devon) in 1891, has some connection with the early conquests of Vespasian. Cp. Ptolemy II. 3. 13. See Haverfield in Arch. Journ. XLIX, pp. 186-181.

2. Freeman, Exeter (Historic Towns Series) p. 11.

must be left to our imagination, masters of southern and central England.[1] The tribes that still remained free were the Dumnonii of Cornwall, the Silures and Ordovices of Wales and the western counties of England, and the Brigantes in the north. But if the influence of the Romans already extended so widely, the sphere of their administrative activity was still restricted to that part of the country south of a line to be drawn perhaps from Camulodunum to Glevum (Gloucester) through Verulamium (St. Albans).[2] North of this line the Iceni and the inland cantons of the Catuclauni, perhaps now fallen under the headship of the Iceni,[3] were only partially subjected to Roman authority, and even south of the line several tribes were still formally autonomous, not to mention the independent clans of the Dumnonii.

For his distinguished services in thus laying the basis of a Roman province in Britain Plautius was honored on his return to Rome in 47 A. D. with permission to enter the city in triumph.[4] Since 26 B. C. no private citizen had won this signal mark of imperial favor, and Plautius was the last to receive it.[5] Nor were the merits of Vespasian forgotten. Returning from Britain with his chief he was decorated with the triumphal insignia.[6]

P. Ostorius Scapula the new governor did not assume his duties until late in 47.[7] He was a man well adapted to handle a half formed province, a strict disciplinarian, a hard fighter and capable of strong initiative. As often happened afterwards in Britain the change of governors was the signal for a general relaxation of discipline among the troops, and renewed activity among the enemy.[8] The legionaries worn

[1]. Tac. Ann. XII. 31 ff. Cp. Mommsen. Prov. I. 192. Furneaux. p. 138.
[2]. Cp. Furneaux p. 138.   [3]. See Merivale VI. 27.
[4]. Dio LX. 30. Tac. Ann. XIII. 32.   [5]. Mommsen, Staatsrecht I. 136. 1.
[6]. Sueton. Vesp. 4.   [7]. Ann. XII. 31. 1.
[5]. Ann. XII. 31. Cp. Agr. 18.

by constant privation and exposure welcomed the chance for a brief indulgence in the pleasures of inactivity. The enemy took advantage of the lateness of the season and the unreadiness of the Romans, to make incursions into the territories of the friendly tribes. The dependent tribes that had not yet resigned themselves to the sway of the fasces were ready to go over to the side of their belligerent compatriots at the slightest encouragement. But Ostorius laid a heavy hand on all these symptoms of disorder, and by his timely and decided action made himself respected by his soldiers and feared by the Britons.[1]

It is hard to say exactly how the Roman army was distributed at this time over the conquered territory. Huebner supposing that the conquest radiated from the harbor of Southampton inclines to place the bulk of the troops in camps south of the Thames. But the progress of the occupation seems to have been from more than one base. That so many Roman roads centred in London can be no chance occurrence. The London stone[2] seems to have had its meaning. The road from Londinium to Calleva probably had as much to do with the conquest of the Atrebates as the road from Venta to Calleva. While a large division of the army may have been in camp at some time in Venta Belgarum (Winchester), it is most unlikely that here was the first great, general camp of 40,000 men.[3] All that can be affirmed with any plausibility is that at most two legions with their auxiliaries camped here, perhaps the Second and Twentieth. These two legions would seem to have been from the beginning assigned to the west, where they afterwards for over two centuries had their

---
[1.] Ann. XII. 31.
[2.] Smith, Dict. Antiq. II. p. 172a. But see Huebner in C. I. L. VII p. 21a.
[3.] Cp. Haverfield in Class. Rev. (1895) p. 236.

standing camps.[1] Vespasian who commanded the second legion subdued the Isle of Wight, and the earliest inscriptions of soldiers of the Twentieth have been found at Bath. On the other hand there is no evidence that either the Ninth or the Fourteenth was at this time engaged in the south. The early inscriptions of these legions set up in places north of the Thames were doubtless destroyed in the insurrection of 61 A. D. which did not extend south of that river.[2] Moreover a large number of troops must have been required from the first to hold down the Trinovantes and Catuelauni, to impress soldiers, and to overawe the Iceni and other northern tribes. The first permanent camp built in Britain, that of the XIV Gemina, may be placed at Camulodunum,[3] and the IX Hispana was surely not far away,[4] perhaps at Verulamium, the old stronghold of Cassivelaunus. The road between Londinium and Verulamium, later prolonged to Venonae and Viroconium, would connect the camp at Verulamium with the supplies and military stores of the mercantile metropolis.

We may with some mental reservation follow Huebner in assuming Glevum to have been the first stationary camp of the II Augusta. Though no inscriptions of any kind have been found at Gloucester, the place abounds in other remains of the Roman city. The form of the camp which contained forty-five acres can still be traced.[5] Uninscribed tiles, pieces of tesselated pavement, arms, pottery, reliefs, etc., have been

---

1. C. I. L. VII, sections 13, 16, 17. Ephem. Epigr. VII, Mommsen, Prov. I. 193.   2. See ch. VII.

3. Huebner, Hermes XVI, pp. 533-534—"The fact that the colonia of Camulodunum established 51 A. D. was unprotected by fortifications is easiest explained by the proximity of a legionary camp."

4. Cp. Ann. XIV. 32; and XII. 40 where the legion not named, probably the ninth (Huebner, Hermes XVI. p. 535) is engaged in the north.

5. See Furneaux p. 138 n. 1. and Huebner's paper "The Roman Glevum" in the Transactions of the Cotteswold Club.

unearthed from time to time. Parts of the Roman walls are said to be still extant. The coins found at Gloucester are chiefly of Claudius, both original and imitated.[1] That no inscriptions have been found commemorating the presence of the Second Augusta at Glevum is perhaps due to its early advance to lasting quarters at Isca (Caerleon).[2]

It is almost impossible even to surmise where the "stativa" of the twentieth legion was situated in 47 A. D. But as this legion seems to have been early employed in the west, its camp may have been at or near Aquae Sulis (Bath). Here it would keep in subjection the Belgic people among whom were the Mendip lead mines, already operated by the Romans in 49 A. D.[3] The actual superintendence however of the gangs of enslaved Britons employed in mining and working the lead was doubtless entrusted to auxiliary cohorts.

The auxiliaries under Ostorius' command, some 30,000 men, foot and horse, were for the most part assigned to particular legions and naturally shared their camps.[4] Detachments of auxiliaries must have been scattered nevertheless in various posts throughout the half pacified country.[5]

Ostorius quickly proved to his troops that he was not to be trifled with. Though the winter had already set in, he took the field with a flying division of light auxiliary infantry, and falling suddenly upon the scattered bands of the enemy which were wantoning in the fields of the dependent allies and friendly tribes, he soon rid the country of them. Then without losing any time in following up his success Ostorius forced the

1. Archaeologia XVIII (1815) p. 120, and Furneaux p. 138 n.1.
2. Haverfield however holds that there is "no evidence that Glevum was ever a fortress proper during the Roman occupation."—Arch. Journ. XLIX, p. 223 n. 2.   3. C. I. L. VII. 1202.
4. Huebner, Hermes XVI p. 548, cites Tac. Hist. I. 59; IV. 62.
5. Ann. XIV. 33, 34; Agr. 16. 1.

Iceni and other northerly tribes which he suspected of collusion with the enemy to give up their arms, and made ready to occupy the whole country south of the Trent River and the Wash, and east of the Severn.[1]

These vigorous measures which plainly aimed at destroying any remnant of freedom in central England caused a great insurrection in which several tribes, the Iceni in the lead, took part. The Iceni had hitherto been fast friends of the Romans. Ostorius attacked them intrenched in a strong position with only his auxiliary troops, and after hard fighting won the victory. The other revolted tribes hearing of the overthrow of the Iceni laid down their arms.[2] Ostorius was now master of the central counties. It was apparently at this time also that the Brigantes, the great tribe north of the Trent, under their queen Cartimandua made some sort of submission to the Roman governor.[3] Perhaps the ninth legion was now moved into quarters at Venta Icenorum (Norwich), to make sure that Prasutagus should conduct himself properly for the future. These events seem to have taken place before the close of 47.[4]

Next year the Romans advanced into the territory of the Decangi, a tribe of north Wales, probably located in Flint and Cheshire.[5] The Decangi did not dare meet the Romans in the field. Ostorius was engaged in wasting and plundering the land, and had

---

1. Tac. Ann. XII. 31. 2 cunctaque cis Trisantonam (the emendation of Heraeus supported by Bradley). See Furneaux' note. Bradley's reading does less violence to the MS. text than any other. *Cuncta* is a broad word, not to be satisfied with the establishment of a single camp (*castris*), nor with the interpretation of Trisantona Tern. The advance to the Trent moreover alone furnishes a meaning for the sudden reversal of attitude on the part of the Iceni. Haverfield now assents to Bradley's view. See his paper in the Chester Archaeological Journal Vol. V. Pt. I (1893) p. 103.
2. Ann. XII. 32. 1.
3. XII. 32. 3 prioribus firmatis.
4. Ostorius still has only his auxiliaries in the field, XII, 31. 5. Cp. 31. 2.
5. Haverfield in Arch. Journ. XLIX, pp. 221-223.

almost reached the north coast of Wales, when dissensions among the Brigantes, arising no doubt from the hostility of the anti-Roman element to their pro-Roman queen, called him back. His intervention and punishment of the disaffected restored order and the supremacy of Cartimandua.

The Silures next engaged Ostorius' attention. Finding that he could do nothing with them by either violence or diplomacy, Ostorius resolved to push forward into their territory and plant legionary camps there.[1] But before doing so he settled a colony of veterans, the colonia Victricensis, at Camulodunum, which should be the capital and central garrison of the established province.[2] Here a temple was erected to the emperor Claudius, intended to be like the altar of Augustus at Lugudunum (Lyons) the centre of the provincial cultus of Rome.[3] The fourteenth legion seems to have been at this time transferred to the west, to take part in the great effort against the Silures.[4]

Driven from point to point by the armies of Plautius, the heroic Caratacus had at last found in the mountainous home of the Silures a stronghold of freedom and barbarian valor which he could hope to defend against his enemy. His romantic fame as a guerrilla leader and as a patriot was a sure passport to the Silures. They made him their commander and their trust in him was increased by many successful fights fought under his leadership.[5]

Caratacus seems to have justified the hopes of the Silures by his skilful conduct of the war during three years 49-51, against the three legions at least under

1. Ann. XII. 32.
2. Furneaux p. 142. Orell. 208. cp. Domaszewski in Rhein. Mus. 1803 p. 345 n. 2. Merivale VI. 32. See also Pliny H. N. II. 77, where the distance to Mona is measured from C.
3. Ann. XIV. 31. cp. Furneaux p. 142.
4. See Mommsen Prov. I. 193. Meyer, in Philologus XLVII, p. 659.
5. Ann. XII. 33.

Ostorius, and the auxiliary forces in addition. Almost no details of this war have been described by Tacitus, but that Caratacus held his own against the Romans for three years, baffling all the military science and dashing enterprise of Ostorius, proves how nobly the British prince had borne his misfortunes and how, taught by experience and adversity, he closed his career even more gloriously than it had begun. He appears after a period of indecisive warfare to have drawn Ostorius off to the territory of the Ordovices in northern Wales. In the year 51[1] he had once more brought about a coalition of tribes against the Romans. Rendered confident perhaps by his successes and by the increased numbers of his army, and perhaps tired of the slow monotony of guerrilla warfare, Caratacus now ventured a pitched battle.

He chose a very strong position somewhere in the Welsh mountains. The Roman army advanced furiously to the attack, though Ostorius himself had at first hesitated. The consciousness of superiority in men who had not known defeat in open fight bore down all resistance. The victory of the Romans was complete. Caratacus' wife, daughter and brothers fell into the hands of Ostorius. He himself fled to Cartimandua queen of the Brigantes, and was promptly delivered in irons to the Roman governor.[2]

The people in Italy were eager to see the man who had defied their armies for so many years. Caratacus was brought to Rome, and after being exhibited in the Campus Martius with his wife, daughter and brothers, received the emperor's pardon. The senate indulged in some chatter about former illustrious captives, comparing Claudius to P. Scipio and L. Paulus. Triumphal insignia were granted to Ostorius.[3] The emperor

---

1. Ann. XII. 36. 1.   2. Ann. XII. 33-36.   3. Ann. XII. 38.

magnified himself and smiled royally on the boom in statues and arch-building.

But in the meantime the Silures driven to desperation by the downfall of the coalition in northern and central Wales suddenly assailed a Roman camp which had been built in their territory (probably at Isca) and was garrisoned by some legionary cohorts. The Roman force narrowly escaped annihilation. Ostorius was now in failing health, worn out by his prolonged exertions, anxieties, and exposure to the rains and cold of four campaigns in a wild, comfortless country. But he continued to prosecute with feverish energy a war of extermination against the stubborn Silures. At the last, though he seems to have kept his hold on Isca, his declining powers became apparent in a series of small disasters. When Ostorius died, the cause of the Silures had become so prosperous that they were inducing some tribes to revolt, and the province might at any time be at their mercy.[1]

The successor of Ostorius, A. Didius Gallus, made a quick journey to Britain, but probably did not arrive there before the beginning of 52 A. D.[2] In the meantime a legion under Manlius Valens suffered a defeat from the Silures and the enemy was ravaging Roman territory. Didius already an old man had a great reputation as a general.[3] But he was also a statesman, and though his peaceful policy, so necessary for the organization of the province, was distasteful to a paper warrior like Tacitus, it was Didius who changed Roman Britain from a great military camp to something more like a regularly administered province. After driving the Silures back into their fastnesses, the governor refrained from further conquest and devoted his five

[1]. Tac, Ann. XII. 38-39.
[2]. Ann. XII. 40. cp. Huebner in Rhein. Mus. 1857 p. 48.
[3]. Ann. XII. 15 ; 40.

years' administration to the consolidation of the province.[1] Besides a slight, perfunctory advance of outposts, the only act of aggrandizement attributed to him was an armed interference in the civil war between Cartimandua queen of the Brigantes and her consort Venutius. Cartimandua was rescued from extreme peril, but Venutius retained the sovereignty over part of the Brigantes.[2] In the west Isca was held as an advanced post among the Silures, possibly garrisoned by detached cohorts, and not yet by the II Augusta which remained at Glevum.[3] Viroconium also dates from the wars of Ostorius as an outpost against the Ordovices, occupied it may be by the fourteenth and twentieth legions.[4] The ninth legion may on the occasion of the Brigantian trouble under Didius have been moved forward from Venta Icenorum to Lindum (Lincoln).[5]

The quiet rule of Didius gave a great impulse to commerce, to the immigration of merchants, artizans, laborers and other Roman or Romanized inhabitants of the empire, and to the working of the lead mines in the Mendip Hills of Somersetshire.[6]

Britain was perhaps the most productive mineral territory belonging to the Romans except Spain.[7] It was soon found necessary to limit the annual output of lead by law.[8] For some unaccountable reason the valuable tin mines of Cornwall do not seem to have been discovered and worked until a late period of the

---
1. Ann. XII. 40. 7 "per ministros agere" indicates the development of bureaux of administration. 2. Tac. Hist. III. 45; Ann. XII. 40.
3 Ann. XII. 32; 38. cp. Mommsen Prov. I. 193 and Huebner in Hermes XVI. p. 530-533.
4. C. I. L. VII. 154.155. cp. Mommsen Prov. I. 193 and Domaszewski, Rh. Mus. (1893) p. 342.
5. Cp. Ruggiero Diz. Epigr. Vol. I. 103c b.
6. Ann. XIV. 33. Dio. LXII. 8. 1. C. I. L. VII. 1201 ff.
7. Cp. Cox, Arch. Journ. 1895 p. 26.
8. Pliny H. N. XXXIV. 49.

occupation.[1] But the lead and iron mines of Somersetshire and the iron of Gloucestershire must have been very extensively worked under the government of Didius Gallus.[2] The revenues of these mines were appropriated by the emperor for his patrimonium or private purse.[3] The Britons who were found working the mines now toiled for the profit of their masters.[4] Roman metallurgic science vastly increased the output of lead and iron, and from some of the lead much silver was extracted

Didius constructed and improved many roads, for example from Londinium to Viroconium, Glevum to Isca, Glevum to Viroconium, etc. These roads were of course built for military purposes rather than as avenues of trade. Forests began to be cut down and marshes drained, in great part by enforced British labor, in order to clear the ground for roads and agriculture.[5] The Britons of the interior were taught to put their trust in crops as well as in flocks and herds.[6] Fruit-trees were introduced.[7] Glass and pottery manufactures began to be carried on by Roman citizens in the towns of the southeast.[8] This part of the island was now so thoroughly pacified that the tribes south of the Thames, perhaps sharing the prosperity of Cogidubnus as traditionally good subjects, did not revolt with the rest of Britain in 61 A. D.

Londinium was among the most thriving commercial cities of the empire. Farther west Aquae Sulis had already become famous for its mineral waters. Baths

1. Haverfield, Arch. Journ. XLIX, p. 178.
2. C. I. L. VII. 1201 ff. cp. Cox, Arch. Journ. 1895 p. 33. Edwards in "Social England" I. 86.
3. Marquardt, Staatsverwaltung II. 259. There is no evidence that any British mines belonged to private individuals.
4. Tac. Agr. 31 metalla quibus exercendis reservemur.
5. Agr. 31. 6. Ann. XIV. 38. 3. Agr. 19.
7. Pliny H. N. XV. 30.
8. C. I. L. VII. 1336. cp. Richards in Traill's Social England I. p. 92.

began to be constructed. Some of the earliest Romano-British inscriptions found at Bath show how invalided soldiers came here to recruit their health.[1] A temple tended by native priests was erected in honor of Minerva Sulis the healing goddess of the place.[2] Verulamium (St. Albans) was already a busy, prosperous town. At Camulodunum the veteran colonists made up for their twenty years of hard work by importing all the luxuries and vices that they could afford. They made a shameful abuse of their power over the natives. Those of substance and industry they plundered, while they enslaved the poor and the worthless, doubtless assisted by the blandishments of the wine-jar.[3] A theatre supplied these weatherbeaten, grim old soldiers with the amusements which they appreciated and enjoyed.[4]

It seems unlikely that any provincial diet like that of the Gauls at Lugudunum was yet instituted in Britain. If anything of the kind was ever tried in a province whose inhabitants in general never became Romanized, the assembly must have been at Camulodunum the political centre of Roman Britain. Here at all events was the temple of Claudius symbolizing the omnipresent power of the Roman emperor. The Britons were forced to behold with sadness how the might of their war god Camulus had been brayed by the resistless hammer of the earthly deity at Rome. This temple of which the richest natives were forced to become priests, was a perpetual reminder to the surrounding population of their subjection to an alien race.

The work of Didius Gallus, ignored by Tacitus and other "drum and trumpet historians," was of no mean order. He seems to have been strongly possessed by the civilizing instinct which was beginning to actuate

---

1. C. I. L. VII. section 9. 2. C. I. L. VII. 38-39.
3. Ann. XIV. 31. Agr. 16 "vitiis blandientibus." Cp. Newman in "Social England" I. 112. 4. Ann. XIV. 32.

THE BUILDING OF THE PROVINCE. 89

the Romans, and to which Pliny the Elder gave expression.[1] It was natural for a cultivated, systematic Roman to love order and justice for their own sake. To introduce immediately perfect justice and humanity into the administration was impossible, but Didius at least made it possible for the civilians of the toga to live and grow rich in Britain.[2] If he and his successors had been able to curb the rapacity of the procurator, the usurers, the subactores and all the army of officials who fed upon the substance of the conquered people, such a rebellion as that of 61 might never have take place, and Britain with its mineral and agricultural resources might very soon have become a secure and flourishing province in spite of its isolation and northern climate.

The next governor of Britain, Q. Veranius Nepos, though far advanced in years[3] was still full of martial vigor. Taking charge of a province and an army in splendid condition as a result of Didius' good rule, he proceeded immediately to reduce the Silures. But the aged soldier was not equal to the hardships of British campaigning. Before he could inflict any serious blow upon the enemy he died with a military reputation unimpaired, leaving a rather boastful statement in his will that if he had lived two years longer he would have conquered for Nero the whole province.[4] The administration of Veranius lasted less than a year.[5]

C. Suetonius Paulinus the new governor entered upon his duties in the year 59. Paulinus was popularly reckoned at this time as the only rival of Corbulo for military honors.[6] He had distinguished himself in the Mauretanian war of 42[7] and probably elsewhere since then. Nero's minister Burrus could not have made a better choice of a commander who should realize the

---
1. H. N. XXX. 4. cp. Cic. pro Balbo 43. Lucan I. 450.   2. Ann. XIV. 33.
3. If he was as Jacob thinks the friend of Germanicus See Ann. II. 56.
4. Ann. XIV. 29. 5. Agr. 14. 6. Ann. XIV. 29; H. H. 31. 7. Dio LX. 9.

dream of a Roman Britain by the final subjugation of the hostile tribes.

During the first two years of his command, Paulinus was very successful against the Ordovices and Silures.[1] It was at this time apparently, if not earlier, that the double camp of the twentieth and fourteenth legions was advanced from Viroconium to Deva.[2] This was a good strategic move. At Deva these two legions were in a position to coerce not only the Ordovices but also the Brigantes to the north of the Dee, as the IX Hispana in the east at Lindum controlled both the Brigantes and the Iceni. The II Augusta was perhaps now planted at Isca Silurum (Caerleon), where it remained for two hundred years.[3]

Paulinus was so confident in his new basis at Deva that in the year 61, leaving part of the XX V. V. to hold the camp, he conducted an expedition to the island of Mona (Anglesey), which was a favorite refuge place for his enemies.[4] Separated from the mainland by a narrow strait, the refugees who were very numerous felt themselves comparatively safe from pursuit. It appears also that Mona contained a sanctuary especially venerated by the tribes of this region. The Roman governor perceived that if he could cross the strait there would be no difficulty in overcoming the demoralized crowd cooped up in the island, and finally cutting off any appearance of safety that Mona as an island and sanctuary might present to the tribes on the mainland. There was besides a prospect of considerable plunder, as the fugitives would certainly carry with them any small articles of value which they might possess. Paulinus had flat-bottomed boats constructed to convey the infantry across. The cavalry forded and swam their

---

[1]. Agr. 14. [2]. Cp. Domaszewski, Rhein. Mus. 1893 p. 342 ff.
[3]. Agr. 14 firmatisque praesidiis. C. I. L. VII. Sect. 13.
[4]. Agr. 14; Ann. XIV 29.

way over. A disorderly mob of men, women and children, many perhaps clinging with a last hope to the rude, blood-stained altars of their gods, could offer no resistance to the legions. A general massacre took place. The island was ravaged and the sacred groves of the oak hewn down. Suetonius might now assure himself that the conquest of the Ordovices was achieved and that the end of the Silurian resistance must soon come. But as he was engaged in finishing the ruin of Mona, news came to him of a most formidable insurrection close to the very heart of the Roman dominion in Britain, which seemed to threaten the expulsion of the Romans and the triumph of the national cause. The governor hurried away from Mona and with all the men whom he could gather took the road to Londinium.[1]

1. Ann. XIV. 30. Huebner misled by the false statement "praesidium impositum" imagines that part of the XX V. V. was left to garrison Mona. Impossible on the face of it, this supposition is not helped by Agr. 18 "cuius possessione revocatum Paulinum."

CHAPTER VII.

THE REBELLION AND THE FINAL ESTABLISHMENT OF THE PROVINCE.

The eagerness of Suetonius Paulinus to rival the military exploits of Corbulo seems to have made him overlook the growing signs of disaffection among the eastern tribes. Hard by the centre of Roman power was fermenting the long pent up indignation of a proud and virile people ill brooking the change from their barbaric freedom to the systematic levy, the regulated taxation and the other cast-iron forms of civilized Rome. When this new, unbending order was enforced with cruelty and violence, and the natives were exposed to injury and oppression of all kinds, both from public officials and from the soldiers, the condition of the conquered became unbearable.[1]

But Paulinus without due regard to the internal stability of his province continued to move the legions farther away from the centre. The Ninth had presumably been pushed forward already under Didius to Lindum.[2] Paulinus as we have seen established the new legionary camps at Isca and Deva. At Camulodunum the colony of veterans given up to happy indulgence insulted and dispossessed the wealthier natives, and generally conducted themselves in an arrogant, lawless manner, backed by the sympathy of the army which looked forward to the same license after their term of service. The colony, which should have served as a more or less efficient garrison of the capital, lived in thoughtless security, unprotected by any adequate fortifications and altogether unorganized for

1. Agr. 15. Ann. XIV. 31. Dio LXII. 2*ff*.　　2. See above p. 86.

defence.¹ The whole military strength of the government was therefore with the exception of a few posts of auxiliary troops² distributed along the frontiers of the province, before the internal parts were fully reconciled to the new regime.

Paulinus bent on conquest of fresh territory left the procurator Decianus Catus and the minor civil officials full scope for the gratification of their avarice. Roman capitalists loaned money to the Britons at exorbitant rates of interest.3 Evictions commonly followed failure to pay.4 It was inevitable that a highly civilized race would find numberless means not strictly dishonest or unjust of outwitting and overreaching the barbarians. Catus was following the usual Roman custom of reclaiming lands granted to chieftains, for the imperial fiscus.5 Confiscation of property was frequently resorted to under Nero, and was probably not neglected by the procurator as a means of raising revenue for the emperor and enriching himself.

The Iceni, among whom must be counted some of the old Catuelaunian cantons, had always been one of the strongest and most independent of the British tribes.6 Though subdued by Ostorius they had kept the semblance of freedom as a "civitas foederata" under the nominal rule of their chieftain Prasutagus. Recently Prasutagus had died, and in spite of his attempt to save the succession for his daughters by naming Nero as co-heir, his kingdom was formally annexed to the province and his queen Boudicca and his daughters were subjected to outrageous treatment, while Roman adventurers and detachments of soldiers seized upon whatever was valuable in the land. Even the dead king's relatives were treated as slaves.7 The

1. Ann. XIV. 32.   2. Agr. 16. Ann. XIV. 33. 4.
3. Ann. XIII. 42. 7. Dio LXII. 2.   4. Agr. 15 eripi domos.   5. Dio. LXII. 2.
6. Ann. XII. 31. cp. Merivale VI. 27.   7. Ann. XIV. 31. 1-4.

Iceni, who were filled with all the intense devotion of a Celtic tribe to its royalty and nobility, enfuriated at the wrongs of their queen, only waited for the call of a leader to rise together and spring at the throats of their opponents.

The other tribes in the vicinity of the Iceni were hardly less ready to revolt. The Trinovantes suffered from the tyranny of the colony planted in their midst. Some of their wealthiest men were chosen to be priests of the temple of Claudius, only to be forced to sacrifice their property.[1] The Brigantes while professing friendship for the Romans saw the meaning of the camps at Deva and Lindum. Some of the Britons may have heard how the Germans years before, though conquered at first, had revolted and thrown off the yoke.[2] Now that Paulinus was far away with his troops in the island of Mona, the opportunity had come for all Britons who had not forgotten the day of freedom, the retreat of the great Julius and the names of Cassivelaunus and Caratacus, to stand together, putting local jealousies aside, and with a mighty effort hurl back the Roman invader once and for all from the last refuge of the Celtic race.[3]

With the romantic feeling of a woman and a masculine daring beyond Zenobia, Boudicca appealed to her people to rally about her and fight for their freedom. The Iceni swore to be revenged upon their oppressors, and rose in great force. Joined by the Trinovantes they marched upon Camulodunum. The veterans who were all unready sent to Decianus Catus the procurator, but two hundred half armed men were all that he could dispatch to their relief. Assailed on all sides the small Roman force shut themselves up in

---

1. Ann. XIV. 31. 6. Furneaux interprets otherwise, but this must be the meaning. Else delecti has no force.

2. Agr. 15. 3. Apr. 15.

the temple of Claudius. In two days the Britons stormed the temple and massacred all the Romans whom they could find.[1] Petilius Cerialis the legate of the ninth legion, marching from Lindum to succor the beleaguered colony, was met by overwhelming numbers of the enemy, lost all the infantry he brought with him, and fled himself with his cavalry back to camp, where he succeeded in defending himself behind the fortifications.[2] If the Brigantes had joined forces with the patriot army, they might easily have destroyed the camp at Lindum. But this powerful tribe following the fatal habit of barbarians in preferring uncertain future troubles to present exertions, stood aloof waiting to see which way things would turn. As usual disunion among their enemies saved the Romans.

The procurator, who had no good to expect from the Britons, fled to Gaul. But in the meantime Paulinus with the fourteenth and part of the twentieth legion, and auxiliaries from posts along the route, added to those regularly attached to the legions, among them the Batavians,[3] was steadily and painfully making his way eastward from Viroconium,[4] through the midst of tribes disaffected and threatening if not actually in open revolt. That he reached Londinium before the rebels is a remarkable testimony to his military ability and to the marching powers of a Roman army, as well as to the excellence of Roman roads. For a moment the governor hesitated whether to defend Londinium or not. It was becoming clear to him that Cerialis and the ninth legion had met with a disaster. Hoenius Postumus the camp-prefect of the II Augusta at Isca (Caerleon) had already disobeyed the summons of Paulinus to leave his camp and join the main force, probably

---

1. Ann. XIV. 32. 2. Ann. XIV. 32. 3. Tac. Hist. I. 59, etc.
4 Ann. XIV. 33. 1. cp. Haverfield, Chester Arch. Journ. Vol. V. Pt. 1 (1893) p. 102 n. 2.

because of the hostile attitude of the Silures and other tribes through whose territory he would have to pass in going to Viroconium or Glevum.[1] Part of the twentieth legion must have been left to hold the camp at Deva. Paulinus' whole force therefore amounted only to about 10,000.[2] And as Londinium was quite defenceless, it was decided to abandon the town with its large and affluent population of Roman citizens, Romanized Britons and Gauls to the mercies of the enemy. The lives of a population of traders were of no high value in military eyes.[3] Only those who entered the ranks of the army escaped the fate which soon overtook the town.[4]

It is perhaps impossible to determine the course taken by Paulinus after leaving Londinium. Most writers have assumed that it was in the direction of Camulodunum. It is not likely that the Romans were so rash as to retreat along the road to Viroconium.[5] And it is perhaps fair to suppose that Paulinus would move northeast, with some faint hope left of effecting a junction with Petilius Cerialis. This is also the only supposition that will explain how his lines of communication with both the camps of the west and the loyal districts south of the Thames were cut off. For the rebels swooped down upon Londinium and Verulamium, killing men, women and children, in all about 70,000, and shut off the approaches to the Thames.[6] If he had been sure of the complete defeat of the ninth legion, it seems most likely that Paulinus would have marched towards Calleva (Silchester) on the chance of establishing some sort of connections with the II

---

[1]. Ann. XIV. 37. For Hoenius see Huebner in Hermes XVI. p. 532 n. 1. The legate of the II Augusta was away from camp, doubtless fighting the Silures.
[2]. Ann XIV. 34.   [3]. Merivale VI. 51.   [4]. Ann. XIV. 33.
[5]. Also, the operations and final battle were surely not far from the territories of the Trinovantes.
[6]. Ann. XIV. 33.

Augusta, the auxiliary detachments of the mining regions, and Cogidubnus of Chichester.

But wherever he was, the Roman general soon found himself obliged by scarcity of provisions to hazard a decisive battle.[1] He drew up his troops on a hill flanked by ravines, with a wood in the rear; the Britons led by their "warrior queen" Boudicca accepted the challenge to battle, coming on in such numbers as they had never yet opposed at one time to the Romans; both Paulinus and Boudicca exhorted their troops to do their utmost, the one side for life, the other for liberty. The contest was never in doubt. The Britons under their brave but incapable leader fought at mere random. The Roman legionaries soon had nothing to do but chase and massacre. Even the women were cut down. It was as Tacitus says like the old-time, thorough-going victories of the republican armies. Eighty thousand Britons are said to have been slain in the battle. Boudicca died soon after, perhaps by her own hand. The camp-prefect of the II Augusta, Hoenius Postumus, fell upon his sword rather than face a court-martial for disobedience to orders.[2]

The war still lingered for a time, but the back-bone of the rebellion was broken. The soldiers of the fourteenth legion, which earned the title of Victrix from this action, were long held in honor as the "Conquerors of Britain."

At Rome the news of the revolt and the massacre aroused horror and consternation. The wisest shook their heads at the wanton waste of men and treasure that was going on year after year in Britain. We are told that Nero, that is Burrus, a very able statesman who at this time conducted the foreign policy,[3] would

---

[1]. Dio LXII. 8.
[2]. Ann. XIV. 34-37. Young Agricola, afterwards governor of Britain, was with Paulinus. See Tac. Agr. 5.   [3]. Cp. Schiller I. 348.

have abandoned the island but for fear of seeming to cast a reflection on the work of Claudius.[1] If as Schiller thinks[2] it was only at the beginning of his reign that Nero's ministry thought to withdraw from Britain, it is clear that even before the insurrection which practically wrecked the beginnings of Roman life north of the Thames, level-headed men deplored the silly expedition of Claudius and wished for some opportunity of abandoning Britain and returning to the policy of Julius Caesar and Augustus.

The only profit derived from Britain consisted in some lead and silver and a few conscripts for the army who could hardly be trusted. The natural drawbacks of a northern climate and a murky atmosphere, as well as the peculiar isolation of Britain, would always hinder a ready flow of emigration across the Straits of Dover. Neither conquest nor voluntary migration tends northward. Therefore while the light of an exotic civilization was already glimmering unsteadily in the south-eastern part of the island, it could not be expected that the British province would take its place with Gaul and Spain as an organic part of Greater Italy. It was and must long remain a military outpost, and worst of all an outpost against nothing. We cannot believe therefore that if the administration of Nero ever thought of abandoning Britain, the reasons for such a step were not carefully weighed at the time of the insurrection.

Apart from the influence of a young and reckless emperor's aversion to a politic retreat, the considerations which decided the government to retain Britain were perhaps three—(1) The general necessity for a conquering power not to recede; (2) The traditional maxim of Roman warfare never to yield in defeat; (3) The unwillingness of the imperial government to admit the

---

[1]. Sueton. Nero 18.   [2]. Schiller, Nero p. 419 n. 1.

colossal folly of the preceding emperor, closely combined with a fear of the popular judgment.

Fifty years before, when the principate was not yet unshakably established, Augustus had made what he intended to be a temporary evacuation of Germany, after a military occupation as long as that of Britain had been in 61 A. D., in spite of these considerations and in spite of the strategic necessity of adding Germany to the empire, because he feared further disasters and saw that the time was not come for an advance to the Elbe. But the government of Nero having overcome the revolt of the Britons had not the courage to withdraw from a useless and inconvenient possession, a clumsy after-thought of Roman empire-building.

The active revolt like that of the Germans in 9 A. D. seems to have been confined to a small section of the province. But it was just the section in which municipal life had progressed most vigorously under Roman rule. The only towns that had attained to any note, Camulodunum, Londinium and Verulamium were wiped out of existence. It would be a long time before eommercial enterprise, capital and civilian labor would recover sufficiently from the scare to make any considerable ventures away from the Romanized mainland. The over-confidence which had manifested itself since the first years of Didius Gallus' government must now give place to an extreme timidity.

But Suetonius Paulinus did not despair of his province for a moment after his great victory. The tribes which had not yet risen now kept quiet. Reinforcements from the mainland repaired the losses of the IX Hispana and the auxiliaries. New camps were established for auxiliary detachments, to watch disaffected and suspected cantons. Suetonius avenged the massacres with extreme rigor. Lands were laid waste on the slightest provocation. Crops were burnt, and this added to neglect of sowing caused a severe famine, which only rendered the natives more desperate and unwilling to give up fighting.[1]

The successor of Decianus Catus was Julius Classicianus. The new procurator had little to do but criticize and quarrel with the governor.[2] Possibly his instructions were to direct the hatred of the Britons as far as might be against Paulinus personally, in order that their animosity against the Roman race as a whole might lose some of its intensity. However that may be, his complaints of the governor's cruelty and vengeful fury seem to have been partially justified. Paulinus had not made himself popular with the provincials. The *annona*, or contributions of grain, weighed more heavily upon them since the vigorous renewal of hostilities on the frontiers. And in the bloody suppression of the rebellion, Paulinus had come to appear to them as the very incarnation of tyranny and brutality. The new procurator therefore made frequent representations to the home government that unless Paulinus were superseded, order could never be restored to the country except with the extinction of its inhabitants.[3]

Accordingly Nero sent Polyclitus, one of his freedmen, to investigate the troubles. Polyclitus cleverly avoided disputes with the governor or the procurator, and after patching up some sort of understanding between them, returned without openly recommending the removal of Paulinus. However a pretext was shortly afterwards found for relieving him of his command and installing Petronius Turpilianus in his stead.[4]

Under Petronius (62-65) the province of Britain was strongly re-established, without attempt at extension of

1. Ann. XIV. 38.   2. Ann. XIV. 38.
3. Ann. XIV. 38.   4. Ann. XIV. 39.

territory already gained.¹ On his return to Rome in 65 A. D., the governor was granted the triumphal insignia.² The work of pacification and reconstruction begun by Petronius was so well advanced under his successor, Trebellius Maximus (65-68)³ that Nero did not fear to withdraw the redoubtable fourteenth legion for the Albanian war,⁴ and the island province easily weathered the storms of 68-69 A. D.

The Britons dwelling within the limits of the province governed by Paulinus never, so far as is known, rose again against Roman rule. Even in 69, when the fall of the last Caesar and the rival claims of great leaders to his inheritance seemed about to wreck the well built empire of Augustus, when the call of the Druids was awakening in the Gallic Celts strange memories of past glory,⁵ when the violence of the three British legions had forced Trebellius Maximus to flee his province,⁶ and when large detachments of the II Augusta, XX V. V. and IX Hisp. were called away to fight for Vitellius in Italy,⁷ the British subject showed no sign of exchanging the hoe for the claymore and asserting his old freedom.⁸ The same quiet continued under the feeble rule of Vitellius' lieutenant, Vettius Bolanus (69-71),⁹ though the Gauls were up in arms, leagued with Civilis in a dangerous revolt against the new principate of Vespasian, and the XIV was again withdrawn—this time not to return—along with detachments of the II Augusta, for active service on the Rhine.¹⁰ There was no druidic organization in Britain to stir up the people to rebellion. We hear not even of any individual priest who felt himself called to the work

1. Agr. 16. 2. Ann. XV. 72. 3. Agr. 16.
4. Tac. Hist. II. 11 ; II. 66. 5. Tac. Hist. IV. 54.
6. Hist. I. 60. 7. Hist. II. 97 ; III. 22.
8. Hist. IV. 54 " fingebantur." Hist. III. 45 is only an ignorant repetition of part of Ann. XII. 40. 9. Agr. 16. Hist. II. 65.
10. 70 A. D. Hist. IV. 68. See Mommsen in Hermes XIX, pp. 439-441.

of lifting an oppressed nation out of bondage. What religion the Roman military professed and promoted was not essentially so far from identical with the old Celtic beliefs that the British leaders should deem a Holy War feasible.

While the established province remained submissive, the Silures and other tribes to the west and north continued to give annoyance to the Roman governors. Petilius Cerialis (71-75), Frontinus (75-78) and Agricola (78-85 had to wage an aggressive war of defence almost continuously with the Silures and Brigantes.[1] It was only under the command of the great Agricola that these tribes were reduced to anything like subjection, and incorporated in the actual province.[2] Still, these generals had a great advantage over Paulinus in that they operated with an assured basis in southeastern Britain, which gave them a free hand to advance the frontiers of a settled and established province.[3]

Unfortunately, our authorities both books and stones give us practically no information about the period of industrial stagnation and slow recovery which followed the rebellion of 61. It is possible that Camulodunum never regained its position of primacy,[4] and that for a time Londinium,[5] but eventually Eburacum[6] became the capital of the province. Mining was doubtless carried on with increased activity, by means of the forced labor of many refractory natives.[7] But exports to Britain and products manufactured there must have been restricted for a time to barely the articles in demand for the public service and the army.[8] Similarly

1. Agr. 17.   2. Agr. 18, 20.
3. Pfitzner (Jahrbb. f. class. Phil. CLIII, pp. 560-564) would have it that Agricola crossed to Ireland. But see Haverfield in C. R. VIII p. 325; IX p. 310; XI p. 447.
4. See scarcity of epigraphic remains.   5. Huebner in C. I. L. VII. p. 21a.
6. Huebner in C. I. L. VII, p. 61a.
7. Cp. Agr. 31. Plin. H. N. XXXIV. 49. See C. I. L. VII. n. 1204.
8. e. g. for the army, cheap pottery and glassware, tiles, liquors, etc.

there is nothing to show that immigration to the new province was anything but extremely meagre, perhaps confined to the hangers on of the army, the mechanics, artizans, amusement mongers, potters, pedlars of various description, cobblers, etc.

But in fact the real Roman municipal life never took root in Britain.[1] Its isolation, its distance from Italy, its climate, and later, when the province had begun to be of more value to the empire, as a wool and grain-growing country,[2] the ferocity and dangerous restlessness of the non-subject tribes were enough to scare away the ever more timid subject of the empire. The vast mass of the British people themselves worked peacefully with their cattle and flocks and fields, and paid their tithes which grew heavier and heavier as the empire sank into bankruptcy. Some labored in the mines, or made roads and drains; some hunted or fished; some joined the army; some few perhaps rose to a certain prominence in their own country. But it was a humble part that the British subject of Rome played in the political, moral and intellectual development of the world. The whole period of the Roman occupation was for the natives one of moral paralysis and soullessness. The establishment of the British province, so useless to the Romans, inaugurated moreover the only lifeless and uneventful epoch in the domestic history of Britain. So far as is known, not a British Celt rose to be emperor of Rome or high in the imperial administration. Not one attained eminence, during the Roman occupation, in letters, or in philosophy, or in the church. In Gaul the Celts forgot their own language and adopted Latin. In Britain the people as a whole neither learned Latin, nor adopted Roman

1. See Haverfield in Arch. Journ. XLIX pp. 188-189, and 215-219.
2. Paneg. Const. Aug. c. 9. Ammian. XVIII. 2.

manners and dress.[1] But they did not therefore inherit the nobleness of their forefathers. Intellectually and morally spineless, the Briton of the Province finally lost much of his splendid physical power, so that he fell stupidly, like a sheep, under the axe of the Saxon. And with the degenerate Britons, the stunted and decaying works of Rome were likewise swept from the face of the land by the new conquerors.

The advance of the Roman armies into Britain and the incorporation of part of that island in the empire can not therefore be defended as a wise or beneficent measure. It was not good, but very bad for Rome. The provincials certainly did not gain, in spite of the introduction of a scientific administration such as the world had not known before. Augustus, Burrus and Domitian saw the British question in its true light. Appian probably voices the opinion of Hadrian when he declares that Britain is unprofitable to the empire. [2] But the toy that Claudius paid so much to get was never let go until the grip of old Rome was broken by her enemies. The sister provinces of Britain rejoiced or acquiesced in the extra effort of maintaining her as an idle member of the family. The Romans, strongly possessed as they were of the economic instinct, set great store by things of a less material order, especially the virtues and powers by which they had overcome the nations, and also the ornaments of empire. They refused to relinquish what was economically useless, by reason of the conquering instinct and a sentimental attachment to a beautiful luxury. And as true sentiment can not long separate itself from utility, it must be confessed that in one instance at least the imperial government allowed itself to be seduced from its best interest by a false and unreasonable sentiment.

1. Cp. Freeman, Norman Conquest I. 19. In spite of Tac. Agr. 21. Note in Gildas, ch. 14, the sharp distinction drawn between Romani and Britanni.
2. Proem. 5.

Latin poets seldom refer to Britain except as a land of savages. Literary men liked to think that there were still lands within the empire where under primitive conditions of life, undisturbed by the conventionalities and complexities of a sham culture, men could be born and grow up strong and rugged. It was apparently a curious mingling of sentimental motives, such as the love of conquest and adventure, and the pride of ownership that led to the establishment of the British province and its long maintenance as part of the empire.

I, WILLIAM FERGUSON TAMBLYN, was born at Oshawa, Ont., 1874. I attended the Whitby Collegiate Institute, and from 1891 to 1895 Toronto University, where I received the degree of B. A., with First Class Honors in Classics. In 1895-6 I studied at the American School of Classical Studies in Rome, under Professor Hale. In the years 1896-7 and 1897-8 respectively, I held the Fellowship in Latin and the Henry Drisler Fellowship in Columbia University.

9 3 1½   6